Leone Levi

Wages and Earnings of the Working Classes

Report to Sir Arthur Bass

Leone Levi

Wages and Earnings of the Working Classes
Report to Sir Arthur Bass

ISBN/EAN: 9783337062309

Printed in Europe, USA, Canada, Australia, Japan

Cover: Foto ©Suzi / pixelio.de

More available books at **www.hansebooks.com**

WAGES AND EARNINGS

OF THE

WORKING CLASSES.

REPORT TO SIR ARTHUR BASS, M.P.

BY

LEONE LEVI, F.S.S., F.S.A.,
OF LINCOLN'S INN, BARRISTER-AT-LAW,
PROFESSOR OF THE PRINCIPLES AND PRACTICE OF COMMERCE IN KING'S COLLEGE, LONDON,
DOCTOR OF ECONOMIC SCIENCE IN THE UNIVERSITY OF TÜBINGEN.

LONDON:
JOHN MURRAY, ALBEMARLE STREET.
1885.

CONTENTS.

CHAPTER I.

	PAGE
THE INCOME OF THE WORKING CLASSES' REPORT	1
Section 1. Number of Earners	2
„ 2. Wages	3
„ 3. Earners and Earnings	4
„ 4. Earners and Earnings in England and Wales, Scotland, and Ireland	5
„ 5. Relation of the Income of the Working Classes' to the Total Income of the People ...	6
„ 6. Relation of Wages to Production	8
„ 7. The Past and the Present of Working Class Earnings	10
„ 8. Other Sources of Working Class Income ...	11
„ 9. The Family Income of the Working Classes ...	12
Supplemental Notes	13
Number of Persons Employed in the Different Occupations	17
Estimated Amount of Earnings	19

CHAPTER II.

ECONOMIC CONDITION OF THE WORKING CLASSES IN 1884 AND 1857.

Section	1. Inquiries into the Condition of the Working Classes	24
„	2. Gradations among the Working Classes ...	25
„	3. Physical Condition of the Working Classes ...	25
„	4. Progress of Education among the Working Classes	27
„	5. Are Our Working Men Less Laborious? ...	28
„	6. Relations of Employers and Employed ...	29

			PAGE
Section	7.	Comparison of Wages, 1857 and 1894 ...	30
,,	8.	Expenditure of the Working Classes ...	31
,,	9.	Moral Effects of High and Low Wages ...	35
,,	10.	The Law of Wages and Profit Sharing ...	36
,,	11.	Investments of the Working Classes ...	38
,,	12.	Prospects of the Working Classes	38
Digest of Proceedings of the Industrial Remuneration Conference ...			40

CHAPTER III.

RECENT CHANGES IN THE DISTRIBUTION OF WEALTH.

Section	1.	Value of Estimates of National Income and National Wealth	44
,,	2.	Estimated Amounts of Income and Wealth ...	44
,,	3.	Changes in the Distribution of Wealth ...	46
,,	4.	Classification of the Population	46
,,	5.	Assessed Incomes of the Middle and Higher Classes	47
,,	6.	Relation of Land to Other Sources of Wealth	50
,,	7.	Incomes of the Lower Middle Classes ...	51
,,	8.	Incomes of the Labouring Classes	52
,,	9.	Population and Income in 1851 and 1881 ...	53
,,	10.	Progress and Poverty	55
,,	11.	Relative Improvement of Different Classes of Society	57

CHAPTER IV.

APPROPRIATION OF WAGES AND OTHER INCOME			59
Section	1.	What has Become of the Increase of Earnings from 1867 to 1883?	59
,,	2.	Consumption of, and Expenditure in, Alcoholic and Non-Alcoholic Beverages	59
,,	3.	Proportionate Personal Expenditure of Working, Middle, and Higher Classes	60
,,	4.	Incidence of Taxation	63

WAGES AND EARNINGS OF THE WORKING CLASSES.

CLASS I.—PROFESSIONAL.

Order	I.	Persons Engaged in the General or Local Government of the Country	73

CONTENTS.

			PAGE
	(a) National Government.		
	Sub-Order 1. Artificers and Labourers in Her Majesty's Dockyards		73
	Post-Office		75
	(b) Local Government—		
	Sub-Order 2. Police		75
Order II.	Persons Engaged in the Defence of the Country—		
	Sub-Order 1. Army		76
	,, 2. Navy		79
,, III.	Persons Engaged in Professional Occupations		80

Class II.—Domestic.

,, IV.	Persons Engaged in Domestic Offices		80
	Sub-Order 1. Domestic Service		80
	,, 2. Other Service		80

Class III.—Commercial.

,, VI.	Persons Engaged in the Conveyance of Men, Animals, Goods, and Messages		81
	Sub-Order 1. Railways		81
	,, 2. Carriers on Roads		83
	,, 3. Carriers on Canals and Rivers		84
	,, 4. Seamen		84
	,, 4. Dock Labourers		87
	,, 4. Warehousemen and Others Engaged in Storage		87
	,, 4. Messengers and Porters		88

Class IV.—Agricultural.

Order VII.	Persons working the Land and engaged in Growing Grain, Fruits, Grapes, and other Products, and attending to Animals		89
	Sub-Order 1. Agriculture in Field and Pasture		89
,, VIII.	Persons engaged about Animals		93
	Sub-Order 1. Fishermen		93
	,, 2. Herd Keepers, Game Keepers		96

CONTENTS.

Class V.—Industrial.

			PAGE
Order	IX.	Persons engaged in Art and Mechanical Products ...	97
		Sub-Order 1. Printers	97
		,, 1. Bookbinders and Bookfolders ...	100
		,, 2. Lithographers	101
,,	X.	Persons working and dealing in Machines and Implements	101
		Sub-Order 1. Machine Tools and Implement Makers	101
		,, 2. Cutlery	103
		,, 3. Watchmakers	104
		,, 3. Philosophical Instrument Makers	104
		,, 6. Musical Instrument Makers ...	104
,,	XI.	Persons working in Houses, Furniture, and Decorations	105
		Sub-Order 1. Builders	105
		,, 2. Cabinet Makers and Upholsterers	108
		,, 3. Wood Carvers and Toy Makers ...	109
,,	XII.	Persons working in Carriages and Harness—	
		Sub-Order 11. Coachmakers	109
,,	XIII.	Persons working in Ships and Boats—	
		Sub-Order 1. Shipbuilders, Shipwrights ...	110
,,	XIV.	Persons working in Chemicals and Compounds—	
		Sub-Order 1. Chemical	111
,,	XV.	Persons working in Tobacco and Pipes	111
,,	XVI.	Persons working in Food and Spirituous Drinks—	
		Sub-Order 2. Malting and Brewing	112
		,, 3. Corn Millers, Bakers, and Confectioners	113
		,, 3. Sugar Refining	113
		,, 3. Chocolate Manufactures	114
,,	XVII.	Persons working in the Textile Fabrics—	
		Textile Fabrics	115
		Sub-Order 1. Woollen Manufacture	117
		,, 2. Silk Manufacture	118
		,, 3. Cotton Manufacture	119
		,, 3. Linen Manufacture	129
		,, 4. Rope Makers	
,,	XVIII.	Persons working on Dress	131
		Sub-Order 1. Boot and Shoe Makers	131

CONTENTS.

		PAGE
Sub-Order 1.	Hat Manufacture	131
,, 1.	Tailors and Shirt Makers	131
,, 1.	Glove Manufacture	132
Order XIX. Persons working in Animal Substances		133
Sub-Order 1.	Soap and Candle Manufacture ...	133
,, 2.	Skinners, Tanners, and Curriers ...	133
,, 2.	Leather Case and other workers in Leather	133
,, 3.	Brush Makers	133
,, 4.	Tanners	134
,, XX. Persons working in Vegetable Substances—		
Sub-Order 1.	Gum, Oil, and Colourmen	134
,, 3.	Sawyers, Coopers, and Turners ...	134
,, 4.	Paper Manufacture	134
,, XXI. Persons working in Mineral Substances		135
Sub-Order 1.	Coal Mining	136
,, 2.	Gas Works	138
,, 3.	Quarrymen	138
,, 3.	Brickmaking	138
,, 4.	Earthenware and Glass	138
,, 7.	Goldsmiths, Silversmiths, Jewellers	140
,, 8.	Iron Manufacture	142
,, 5.	Salt Works	147

APPENDIX—

Prices Paid at Greenwich Hospital, 1740—1865	148
Average Prices of Wheat, Meat, Potatoes, and Coal, 1852--1882	149
Purchase Value of the Sovereign, 1820—1880	150
Paupers in England and Wales, 1840—1883	150
Amount of Deposits in the Savings Banks, 1840-1883 ...	151
Funds in the Friendly Societies	151
,, Industrial and Co-operative Societies... ...	151
,, Building Societies	151

THE INCOME OF THE WORKING CLASSES.

REPORT.

CHAPTER I.

DEAR SIR ARTHUR BASS,

The inquiry I instituted into the wages and earnings of the Working Classes of the United Kingdom in 1867 * and 1879, by desire of your father, the late esteemed Member for Derby, has, I have reason to believe, been helpful in forming a sound opinion on a subject of great interest, and on which Politicians and Economists alike experienced great difficulty. It was not only their large number, but the improved condition of the labouring classes that suggested and sanctioned the extension of the Franchise. And many are the social and economic problems which depend for their solution on the knowledge we possess of the actual means at the disposal of the masses. Since 1867 the population has increased from about 30,000,000 to 36,000,000, and many vicissitudes have occurred in the rates of wages. After a period of unexampled prosperity in Trade, the nation has experienced all the bitter fruit of a protracted depression; the relations between capital and labour have been frequently strained; and an important Conference† is about to be held for the purpose of considering whether the present

* The inquiry was suggested by a speech by Mr. Gladstone at Liverpool, in 1866. Mr. Dudley Baxter's Paper on National Income was read at the Statistical Society in January, 1868.
† See results of the Conference, page 40.

system whereby the products of industry are distributed between the various persons and classes of the community is satisfactory, or, if not, by what means that system can be improved. It is under these circumstances that you have desired me to renew the inquiry into the wages and earnings of the labouring classes, and I have much pleasure in laying before you the results of my investigations.

Section I.—NUMBER OF EARNERS.

As in the former inquiry, I have taken the number of earners in the different industries from the latest Census, though in some instances, as in the case of Merchant Seamen, whose home is on the sea, I had recourse to other documents for ascertaining the number in the receipt of wages. In all cases I have only taken those who come fairly under the designation of "Working Classes" guided in that distinction by the nature of the work in which they are employed, the mode in which they are paid, and the social position they occupy; though the distinction between the lower middle and labouring classes is often very slender. In order to allow for those temporarily ill, or otherwise unable to work, I have taken for my calculation only those under sixty-five years of age. Paupers in workhouses, prisoners, and persons in hospitals were not included in the number engaged in the different occupations. To the number of labourers as given in the Census we should add at least three per cent. for the increase of population in the last three years. But about a similar deduction would have to be made for the number of masters. In 1867 I found the number of workers to be 11,018,000; in 1881 they were 12,200,000. Assuming the Working Classes to comprise seventy per cent. of the population, and with small farmers, crofters, and others to number 26,000,000 persons, or 5,600,000 families,* the 12,200,000 workers give 2·17 earners for every family.

Section II.—WAGES.

The wages paid in the different industries I have obtained from the employers of labour and from the employés themselves in answer to a Circular I issued in 1884, accompanied in most cases with particulars of great value, for which I am greatly indebted; from the rates given in the Miscellaneous Statistics published by the Board of Trade, including data for the year 1883, not yet published, but kindly communicated to me by the head of the Statistical Department; and from the recent labours of Mr. Lord, late President of the Manchester Chamber of Commerce; Mr. Montgomery, of the Manchester Statistical Society; Mr. Jeans, of the Statistical Society; Mr. Vansittart Neale, at the Social Science Congress, &c., whilst I had before me the valuable work on National Income by the late eminent statistician, Mr. Dudley Baxter. The Average Wages are derived from the proportion of labourers earning different wages in the same industries, and the annual amount of earnings I have calculated from information received as to the regularity and continuity of the different kinds of work. In most cases, adult wages commence with the age of majority; but in the case of domestic servants, factory labourers, and others, persons of fifteen years and upwards usually earn full wages. In the case of domestic servants, seamen, and others, the value of board and lodging must be added to the money

* The number of persons to a family was, in 1881, 4·61 in England and Wales, 4 63 in Scotland, and 5·19 in Ireland, giving an average for the United Kingdom of 4·67 persons to a family.

wages. So must the value of all allotments of land to agricultural labourers, and so the value of uniforms, liveries, or other perquisites, wherever given. It should be remembered, also, that more is earned by piecework and overtime than the rates of wages would indicate, and that the total of these items make up a large amount.

SECTION III.—EARNERS AND EARNINGS.

Generally, without pretending to more correctness than a subject so vast and necessarily so complicated admits of, though resting on two well-ascertained factors—the Census of the population, with a complete analysis of the occupations of the people, and the rates of wages actually prevalent and paid in the various industries—the number of earners and the amount of their earnings in 1867 and 1884 may be taken as follows:—

Occupations.	Number of Earners. Founded on the Census for 1861 and 1881.		Amount of Earnings.		Average Earnings.	
	1884.	1867.	1884.	1867.	1884. £ s.	1867. £ s.
Professional	300,000	300,000	£ 16,000,000	£ 10,000,000	53 7	33 6
Domestic	2,400,000	1,700,000	86,000,000	59,000,000	35 17	34 14
Commercial	900,000	700,000	45,000,000	39,000,000	50 0	55 14
Agricultural	1,900,000	2,700,000	67,000,000	84,000,000	35 5	31 2
Industrial	6,700,000	5,600,000	307,000,000	226,000,000	45 16	40 7
	12,200,000	11,000,000	521,000,000	418,000,000	42 14	38 0

Thus with an increase of 10·90 per cent. in the number of earners, there has been an increase of 24·64 per cent. in the amount of earnings, the average earning per head having increased from £38 in 1867 to £42 14s. in 1884, or in the proportion of 12·37 per cent.

Dividing the earners and earnings by age and sex the results are as follows:—

Occupations	Number of Earners.		Amount of Earnings.		Average Earnings	
	1884.	1867.	1884.	1867.	1884.	1867.
			£	£	£ s.	£ s.
Males under 20	1,650,000	1,200,000	29,000,000	23,000,000	17 12	19 3
„ 20 & under 65*	6,530,000	5,900,000	363,000,000	293,000,000	55 17	49 13
Females under 20	1,300,000	1,300,000	30,000,000	27,000,000	23 2	20 2
„ 20 & under 65	2,720,000	2,600,000	99,000,000	75,000,000	36 14	28 18
	12,200,000	11,000,000	521,000,000	418,000,000	42 14	38 0

The total earnings, thus calculated, include the value of board and lodging wherever given. Deducting this item, the amount of money earnings may be estimated at £470,000,000.

Section IV.—EARNERS AND EARNINGS IN ENGLAND AND WALES, SCOTLAND AND IRELAND.

. The earnings of the Working Classes in England and Wales, Scotland and Ireland respectively, are affected by the different occupations of the people.

The Census of 1881 gave the proportion of persons employed as follows:—

Occupations.	England and Wales.	Scotland.	Ireland.
Professional	... 2·49	... 2·57	... 3·84
Domestic ...	... 6·78	... 4·77	... 8·19
Commercial	... 3·77	... 3·57	... 1·38
Agricultural	... 5·31	... 7·28	... 19·17
Industrial	... 24·50	... 25·20	... 13·28
Indefinite	... 57·15	... 56·61	... 54·14
	100·00	100·00	100·00

With a greater prevalence of the Industrial, or the most remunerative labour, in Great Britain, and of the Agricultural, the least remunerative in Ireland, we cannot wonder at the disparity in the amount of earnings in the three kingdoms. The wages of skilled labourers are nearly uniform in Great Britain and Ireland. Not so are

---

* The Census of 1861 gave the occupations of the people at periods of five years of age. The Census of 1881 gave the same at periods of fifteen years—viz.: at 50 and 65 years of age, and not at 60. Hence the differences as compared with the report of 1867.

the wages of unskilled, and especially of Agricultural Labour, the supply of which in Ireland is greatly in excess of the demand. The proportion of earners and earnings was as follows:—

Countries.	Number of Earners.	Amount of Earnings. £	Average Earnings per head. £ s. d.
England and Wales	8,600,000	401,000,000	46 12 6
Scotland	1,500,000	62,000,000	41 6 8
Ireland	1,800,000	42,000,000	23 6 8
United Kingdom (not allocated)	300,000	16,000,000	53 6 8
	12,200,000	521,000,000	42 14 1

The proportion of earners to population was 31·48 per cent. in England and Wales, 39·47 per cent. in Scotland, and 36 per cent. in Ireland, and of the £505,000,000 of earnings of the working classes which can be allocated, 79·40 per cent. fall on England, 12·29 per cent. on Scotland, and 9·31 per cent. on Ireland.

SECTION V.—RELATION OF WORKING CLASS INCOME TO THE TOTAL INCOME OF THE PEOPLE.

The total income of the people is composed of three items, viz., the Income assessed to the Income-tax, embracing all incomes of £150 and upwards per annum; the Income of the lower middle, and other classes below that amount not so assessed; and the earnings of the working classes. These three classes of income stood approximately in 1867 and 1883 as follows:—

	1866-7. £	Per cent. of total.	1882-3. £	Per cent. of total.
Gross amount of property and profits assessed to Income-tax	423,000,000	44·00	613,000,000	47·70
Income of lower and middle classes	120,000,000	12·50	140,000,000	10·90
Earnings of Working Classes	418,000,000	43·50	521,000,000	41·40
	961,000,000	100·000	1,274,000,000	100·00

The incomes of the higher and middle classes appear thus to have increased between the two periods slightly more than those of the working classes. There is reason to believe, on the other hand, that the increase in the income assessed to Income-tax has been greater in the amount assessed on property than in the amount assessed on income. The relative importance of the income of the Working Classes to the total Income in the three kingdoms appears to be as follows:—

TOTAL INCOME OF ENGLAND, SCOTLAND, AND IRELAND.

—	England.	Per Cent.	Scotland.	Per Cent.	Ireland.	Total.
Amount assessed to Income-tax under Schedules A, B, D, and E	£ 476,700,000	£ 49	£ 59,000,000	£ 44	£ 35,500,000	£ 41
Estimated Income of Lower Middle Class	98,000,000	10	14,000,000	11	8,000,000	10
Earnings of the Working Classes	101,000,000	41	62,000,000	45	42,000,000	49
	675,700,000	100	135,000,000	100	85,500,000	100

Any territorial division of the assessments of the Income-tax must of necessity be imperfect, for the large assessments on landed and house properties under Schedule A., and the colossal incomes assessed under Schedule D., are mainly made at head-quarters; the Metropolitan Assessments embrace properties in other parts of the Kingdom, and the income of public companies is spread over a very undefined area. The income thus *apparently* amounting to £1,274,000,000 is the *gross* income of the people, including much that is a simple transfer from hand to hand. The net income of the nation is probably less than £1,000,000,000 per annum. Again, great difference exists between income from productive and income from unproductive industries, between income from labour for the people *at home*, and income from labour in articles of export, which returns with the value of the merchandise exported.

Section VI.—RELATION OF WAGES TO PRODUCTION.

One of the most difficult problems in Industrial Economics is in what proportion the products of labour ought to be fairly distributed between masters and labourers. The question is, indeed, more theoretical than practical, because under the contract of wages, the most convenient relation for masters and men, all things considered as applicable to the great mass of labourers, the workman renounces and the master assumes, for a consideration, all chances of the operation; and because with free competition, and the necessity on the part of the master of utilising any increasing income, by increasing production, the labourer is certain, sooner or later, to derive his full share of the products of labour. In many industries the proportion of wages to production ranges between 20 to 30 per cent. Sir James Caird estimated the gross amount of Agricultural products consumed in the United Kingdom at £12 per head, which, with the present population, would give a total of £432,000,000. Deduct from this amount the value of Agricultural products imported— £157,000,000—the amount produced at home is found to be £275,000,000. The total amount of Agricultural wages, as estimated in this report, is £66,000,000. Therefore, the proportion seems to be 24 per cent. But the proportion differs widely in different districts.*
In the Cotton Industry valuable data exist for arriving at what may be considered the fair remuneration of labour. From Mr. Ellison's reliable statistics I find that in 1871-75, the total value of produce estimated

---

* In the Report of the Royal Commissioners on Agriculture many instances are given of the proportion of the cost of labour to the value of products on a farm. In one instance, in Hampshire, it amounted to 34·34 per cent. in 1875-1879.

by the total amount of exports, plus one-third for home consumption, being £100,400,000, the cost of cotton was £41,500,000, the wages £25,800,000, other expenses £25,300,000, making a total of £92,600,000, leaving £7,800,000 for rent, depreciation, profits, &c. In 1880-82, the cost of cotton amounted to £38,200,000; the wages, as in this report, £28,500,000, other expenses £27,700,000, total £94,400,000, the total value of produce, estimated as above, was £102,400,000, leaving £8,000,000 for rent, depreciation, profits, &c. a sum much under what is required for the maintenance of the industry.*

Economies may be made in what are called "other expenses" but in any case such gross results account for the complaints of cotton spinners and others connected with this large industry. The relation of wages to production must necessarily depend on the proportion between the cost of the raw material, value of capital, and other expenses, and the market value of the commodities pro-

---

* In the 14th Report of the Bureau of Statistics of Labour, Boston, particulars are given relating to 4440 Industrial Establishments of the proportion of wages of labour to the value of products. On a total value of 861,000,000 dols. the amount of wages was 74,700,000 dols., or 26·69 per cent. In Cotton Goods the proportion was 23·24 per cent. In Woollen Goods 16·50 per cent.

The details of the cost of production in 1859-61 and 1881-82 has been kindly supplied by Mr. Ellison, as follows:—

Average of 3 years, 1859-61.		Average of 3 years, 1880-82.	
Cotton consumed, 1,022,500,000 at 6¾d.	£29,290,000	1,426,690,000 lbs. at 6 7-16d.	£38,211,000
Wages, 646,000 operatives at £3,210 per annum	20,995,000	686,000 operatives at £42 per annum	28,812,000
Other expenses than wages in connection with spinning and weaving	7,800,000		10,700,000
Other expenses, than wages, in connection with bleaching, dyeing, and printing	10,000,000		17,000,000
Rent, interest, depreciation, profits, &c.	8,915,000		12,277,000
	£77,000,000		£107,000,000

duced; and it is not always in the power either of masters or labourers to determine at will either the one or the other. Nor is it possible to arrive, in all cases, at the value of labour in relation to the other factors in production. The cost of setting a diamond is small as compared with the value of the precious stone, and a comparatively valueless piece of clay becomes most valuable in the hand of the potter. In goldsmiths' work the wages are higher, because the great intrinsic value of the material employed renders it necessary to raise the workers above temptation; and because, also, the artistic character of the work ranks the workman among those who are in the borderland of the artist and the sculptor.

SECTION VII.—THE PAST AND THE PRESENT OF WORKING CLASS EARNINGS.

In Eden's "State of the Poor" the wages of agricultural labourers are given, in 1793, at 1/5 per day in winter, and 1/9 per day in summer. Now agricultural labourers seldom get less than 2/ or 2/6 per day. At that time the earnings of agricultural labourers were permanently less than their expenditure, and had to be supplemented by doles from the poor rates. Now, unless wasted, they equal if not exceed what is required for legitimate wants, and, if well thrifted, leave a surplus. In 1831 a single hind in Northumberland got 11/ per week; in 1880, 18/. In 1834 a mule spinner in Manchester earned 34/; in 1884, 53/. And a piecer who in 1834 got 4/9, in 1884 got 12/. All through the long range of labourers' wages more or less advance is noticeable, if not in the rates, certainly in the capacity of earning; any difference between the earnings of different labourers in the same industry being, more generally, the results of comparative skilfulness, perseverance in labour, and quickness of movement.

SECTION VIII.—OTHER SOURCES OF WORKING CLASS INCOME.

In estimating the wages and earnings of the labouring classes, I must not omit to state that the number of persons classed in the Census under "Indefinite" occupations, though mainly engaged in family duties, combine with these occasional labour for wages, and it is among these classes that some of the least remunerative wages generally prevail. In a similar manner the incomes from savings must be added. The large number of houses acquired by the Working Classes through Building Societies produce rents which form part of income, whether received or saved. And so do the profits made from the sub-letting of houses. The annual subventions paid by Friendly Societies are so much income to the recipients. So are the interests paid or accumulating from money in the Savings Banks, trustees, or Post Office. The inquiry mainly relating to wages I have necessarily omitted, though not forgotten, that portion of the workmen's incomes which arises from small industries, such as buying and selling commodities on a small scale, all helping to recruit the family income. Though the present depression of trade has already affected, and may still more operate injuriously upon certain industries, its effects hitherto have been more in a diminution of profits than on lessened production, and therefore the results are not so apparent on the total income of the Working Classes. Altogether, in estimating their total income at this moment at £521,000,000, or, less Board and Lodging, £470,000,000, the chances are that I have rather under than overvalued all the items of income.

Section IX.—THE FAMILY INCOME OF THE WORKING CLASSES.

Taking the number of families belonging to the Working Classes at 5,600,000, and the total income at £521,000,000, or, exclusive of food, &c., £470,000,000, we have an average of about 32/ per week per family—a fair amount if equally distributed. But the gradation of incomes among the labouring classes are proportionally as great as among the higher, for whilst in some cases several members of a family are in the receipt of high wages, in other cases there may be only one person earning but a small pittance, and with it the weight of a large family. Nor is the great preservative of the family purse in charge of the head of the household so prevalent as it ought to be. An average does not convey the real condition of the small earner, whilst it understates the real receipts of the well-paid workman. The value of all averages depends on their being the medium towards which the manifold rates are found to be tending. And if I am right in assuming that the income of the great mass of the labouring classes in the United Kingdom averages, even approximately, at as much as 32/ a week per family, I must come to the conclusion that they are in a better economic condition than the labouring classes of any other country.

I have the honour to be, Sir,

Your obedient servant,

LEONE LEVI.

5, Crown Office Row, Temple,
January, 1885.

SUPPLEMENTARY NOTES.

The Circular issued for the purpose of obtaining the current rates of wages, dated June, 1884; as well as the papers herein inserted on "The Economic Condition of the Working Classes," read at the Meeting of the Social Science Association, at Birmingham, in 1884; and on the "Recent Changes in the Distribution of Wealth," read at the Meeting of the British Association for the Advancement of Science, at Southport, in 1883, had reference to the rates of wages in 1882-1884.

As already stated, a languid state of trade and reduced profits had existed for a considerable time, yet production continued at the ordinary rate, and neither the amount of work, nor the rates of wages, had up to the middle of 1884 materially diminished. The continuance of this state of things, however, suggested and necessitated soon after a curtailment of production and the lowering of wages. And thus employment became gradually less certain and continuous as the year ran on. Even since the publication of the main results of this inquiry in December last, the curtailment of the resources of the Working Classes has become more marked and considerable, and a reduction of full 15 per cent. on the rates of wages may be taken to have been made in the principal branches of industry since the receipt of the Returns.

Fifteen per cent. reduction on the total money income of the Working Classes, £470,000,000 in amount would be equal to about £70,000,000. The reduction, however, is by no means general. Domestic servants are not affected by it, and many branches of industry are in a prosperous condition. The depression of trade touches visibly the wages in the Iron and Coal Industries, the Cotton Manufacture, Shipbuilding, and other branches of more or less importance; indirectly it has a powerful effect on Agricultural wages, and more especially it acts on common labourers. Taking the total amount of income from such industries at £200,000,000, a reduction of 15 per cent. is a loss of £30,000,000 a-year, equal to £2,500,000 per month.

The income of a family, comprising on an average 4·67 persons, includes the earnings of an adult artisan or labourer, and of one or two others—wife, son, or daughter—belonging to the household. A reduction of 15 per cent. where made, constitutes a loss of 3s. to 4s. per week in the man's wages, and a proportional reduction in those of the wife or child. In the higher wages the loss may not produce serious results, but in the case of common labourers, and of persons with precarious employment, the reduction implies a considerable diminution of resources, all the more heavy when accompanied by the difficulty of finding employment for any length of time. An evidence that the depression of trade has already exercised an injurious influence on the labouring classes may be found in the diminished rate of Marriages. How urgent to inculcate the virtue of thrift when work and wages are abundant.

Much criticism has been offered on the method and results of this inquiry. It has been objected that the Census returns are imperfect, that the range of observations may have been too limited for generalisation, that the average wages taken appear too high, and that the discrepancies in the results arrived at, by statisticians in the same field, weaken the amount of confidence to be placed upon their value. On these points I venture to make the following remarks:—

1. The Census returns are admitted to be imperfect. We have no Industrial Census, but in the absence of anything better we must take what we have. It was stated in the respective reports that the inquiry in 1867 was based on the Census of 1861, that of 1878 on the Census of 1871, and that in 1884 on the Census of 1881, with allowances for the intervening years. It should be remembered, however, that even with an equal annual percentage increase of population the number of earners in each succeeding Census is larger, the percentage occurring on the larger number.

2. The basis for induction was by no means narrow, for I have not only issued a large number of circulars, but freely used the data supplied by other writers. The rates of wages in the leading industries, moreover, really govern the total income of the working classes, the bulk of workers being connected with Agriculture, Building, Coal and Iron, and the Textile Manufacture.

3. Agricultural wages for men may be as low as from 7s. to 10s. a week in a few Southern Counties in England, and Ireland, generally, however, with piecework, special allowances at harvest and other times and other advantages amounting in the course of the year to an appreciable item, but wages rise to 30s., 40s., and even 60s. and 80s. per week in other industries. The bulk of agricultural labourers earn 2s. 6d. per day, or £37 10s. per annum. The bulk of builders earn, at least, 30s. to 38s. per week, or £75 to £95 per annum. Highly skilled artisans earn 30s. to 40s., less skilled 23s. to 28s., and common labourers 15s. to 20s. per week. The wages of domestic servants, for men, range £20 to £40 per annum; but board and lodging

must be taken to add, at least, 10s. a week, or £26 per annum.

4. The discrepancies in the total amount of income of the working classes as given by the late Mr. Dudley Baxter, Mr. Giffen, Mr. Mulhall, Mr. Jeans, and myself show the difficulties attending such inquiries principally arising from the want of a common basis as to the description of persons to be included under the designation of working classes, what is to be taken as the rate of wage when piecework prevails, the inclusion or exclusion of overtime, the addition of the money value of board, lodging, clothing, allotment of land, and other allowances. Whatever be the accord, however, it must be admitted that in inquiries of this nature we cannot pretend to attain to any nicety of precision, but must be satisfied with as near an approach as possible to the real facts of the case.

March, 1885.

ESTIMATES OF THE EARNINGS OF THE WORKING CLASSES. 17

NUMBER OF EARNERS.

NUMBER OF PERSONS EMPLOYED IN THE DIFFERENT OCCUPATIONS IN THE UNITED KINGDOM, 1881.

Order.		OCCUPATIONS.	MEN.		WOMEN.		TOTAL.
			Under 20 years.*	20 to 65 years.	Under 20 years.*	20 to 65 years.	
1	1	H. M. Dockyards...	...	18,500	...	...	18,500
1	1	Post Office, Letter Carriers	...	14,300	...	2,700	17,000
1	2	Police	...	53,000	...	...	53,000
2	1	Army	...	182,000	...	...	182,000
	2	Navy	5,000	51,500	...	...	56,500
4	2	Domestic Servants	63,000	224,000	652,000	1,012,000	1,951,000
		Other Services ...	400	17,000	2,400	412,600	432,400
6	1	Railways	23,300	140,000	...	...	163,300
	2	Carriers on Road	24,300	174,000	100	900	199,300
	3	Carriers at Sea ...	45,000	327,000	1,200	2,500	375,700
	4	Warehousemen ...	4,300	25,600	100	3,700	33,700
	5	Messengers, Telegraph	99,500	58,200	1,800	4,600	164,100
7	1	Agricultural Labourers	380,800	1,027,100	37,600	81,000	1,526,500
		Small Farmers ...		300,000	...	...	300,000
8	1	Attending to Animals	9,300	46,600	...	100	56,000
9	1	Printers	23,500	45,300	2,000	1,000	71,800
		Lithographers ...	1,800	5,900	200	100	8,000
	2	Bookbinders ...	2,800	8,100	6,600	6,600	24,100
10	1	Engineers ...	6,900	37,700	...	300	44,900
		Machinists ...	26,800	119,500	100	800	147,200
	2	Implement Makers	7,400	32,000	1,400	7,000	47,800
	3	Watch Makers ...	3,900	20,500	300	600	25,300
	4, 7	Scientific Instrument Makers ...	4,200	24,700	300	1,000	30,200
		Type Cutters, &c.	1,300	5,100	500	1,600	8,500
		Builders	109,600	626,500	..	...	736,100
	2	Cabinet Makers & French Polishers	12,000	55,200	2,800	8,500	78,500
	3	Locksmiths, Gasfitters	3,900	16,400	200	200	20,700
		Wood Carvers & Gilders	2,200	11,700	1,400	3,600	18,900
12	1, 2	Coach Makers & Saddlers	16,200	79,000	700	1,300	97,200
13	1	Shipwrights, &c. ...	9,100	52,700	...	100	61,900
	3	Sailmakers ...	1,000	4,000	...	...	5,000
		Sugar Refiners, Mustard, &c. ...	1,700	6,200	400	800	9,100
14	3	Chemical Manufacturers	1,900	14,100	900	700	17,600
		Carried forward ...	891,100	3,813,400	713,000	1,554,300	6,981,800

* Of those under 20 years of age about three-fourths were from 15 to 20 years.

B

ESTIMATES OF THE EARNINGS

NUMBER OF PERSONS EMPLOYED—*continued*.

Order.		OCCUPATIONS.	MEN.		WOMEN.		TOTAL.
			Under 20 years.	20 to 65 years.	Under 20 years.	20 to 65 years.	
		Brought forward...	891,100	3,813,400	713,000	1,554,300	6,981,800
15	1	Tobacco	11,900	2,900	5,800	5,100	25,700
16	2	Maltsters&Brewers' Cellarmen ...	3,700	38,600	100	600	43,000
		Milk Sellers ...	4,700	19,600	1,200	5,800	31,300
		Corn Millers ...	4,200	24,600	400	100	29,300
		Bakers & Confectioners	23,500	44,200	6,000	18,100	91,800
		Greengrocers ...	1,900	20,600	1,200	3,100	26,800
17	1	Woollen Manufacture	34,600	77,000	58,600	89,400	259,600
	2	Silk Manufacture	4,300	14,900	13,700	28,200	61,100
	3	Cotton Manufacture	82,300	150,700	148,700	237,200	618,900
	4	Flax, Linen,&Hemp Manufacture ...	16,700	42,800	35,300	42,800	137,600
	5	Weavers, Dyers, Factory Hands ...	10,300	24,300	19,200	34,100	87,900
	5	Felt Carpet, &c. ...	2,700	10,000	5,400	10,200	28,300
18	1	Hosiery, Glove Buttons	3,700	18,900	10,800	30,700	64,100
		Hatters, Straw Hats	3,100	13,700	9,500	27,800	54,100
		Tailors, Milliners...	30,000	117,000	131,800	375,800	654,600
		Shirt Manufacture	300	1,400	31,600	118,200	151,500
		Boots, Shoes, Patten Clogs ...	32,900	182,600	12,800	25,300	253,600
		Hair Wig Makers	3,600	13,400	200	600	17,800
		Shawl Manufacture	...	2,200	300	600	3,100
		Umbrella Makers	1,000	3,700	1,800	2,900	9,400
19	1	Tallow, Soap,& Glue Manufacture ...	1,700	9,700	700	900	13,000
	2	Furriers, Tanners, Curriers, Leather	5,400	31,800	1,800	4,100	43,100
	3	Hair Brush, &c. ...	2,200	8,600	2,200	4,900	17,900
20	1	Oil Millers ...	1,700	8,900	100	400	11,100
		Floor Cloth, Japanners,India Rubber	1,800	7,400	1,500	2,100	12,800
	2, 3	Willow, Cane, Timber Sawyers ...	15,200	93,400	2,500	4,800	115,900
	4	Paper Manufacture, Envelopes, Cards, &c. ...	7,900	24,400	13,900	19,900	66,100
21	1	Miners	127,300	378,100	...	...	505,400
	2	Quarrymen ...	9,200	54,600	...	...	63,800
		Slate and Lime ...	2,900	12,600	...	100	15,600
		Brick and Tile ...	11,400	37,400	1,300	1,800	51,900
	3	Paviours, Platelayers	1,800	38,700	...	...	40,500
		Carried forward ...	1,355,000	5,352,200	1,231,400	2,649,900	10,578,400

OF THE WORKING CLASSES.

NUMBER OF PERSONS EMPLOYED—continued.

Order.		OCCUPATIONS.	MEN.		WOMEN.		TOTAL.
			Under 20 years of age.	20 to 65 years.	Under 20 years.	20 to 65 years.	
		Brought forward...	1,355,000	5,352,200	1,231,400	2,649,900	10,578,400
		Railway Labourers	3,400	38,200	100	200	41,900
	4	Earthenware and Glass	7,100	37,700	9,000	11,600	65,400
	5, 6	Salt and Waterworks	500	6,400	...	300	7,200
	7	Goldsmiths and Lapidaries ...	5,300	19,700	2,500	3,900	31,400
	8	Blacksmiths and Whitesmiths ...	26,500	121,300	100	300	148,200
	9	Iron Manufacture, Nails, and Anchors	47,100	202,200	3,300	8,400	261,000
	9, 12	Metal Manufacture	28,000	83,300	7,000	7,500	125,800
22	1	Costermongers ...	4,000	26,500	2,000	17,800	50,300
	2	General Labourers	151,200	588,000	2,400	9,800	751,400
	2	Other Artisans ...	26,200	117,000	14,400	20,100	177,700
23	1	Refuse Matters ...	1,600	12,600	500	1,900	16,600
			1,655,900	6,605,000	1,272,700	2,731,700	12,265,300

ESTIMATED AMOUNT OF EARNINGS.

Order.		OCCUPATIONS.	MEN.		WOMEN.		TOTAL.
			Under 20 years.	20 to 65 years.	Under 20 years.	20 to 65 years.	
			£	£	£	£	£
1	1	H.M. Dockyards...	...	1,200,000	...	...	1,200,000
1	1	Post Office, Letter Carriers	...	850,000	...	150,000	1,000,000
	2	Police	...	*3,600,000	...	...	3,600,000
2	1	Army	...	*7,000,000	...	...	7,000,000
	2	Navy	100,000	*2,900,000	...	...	3,000,000
4	2	Domestic Servants	*1,259,800	*12,344,500	*15,481,000	*39,431,000	*68,516,300
		Other Services ..	*46,500	*628,800	*50,400	*16,628,800	*17,354,500
6	1	Railways	562,000	8,106,000	...	...	8,668,000
	2	Carriers on Road...	607,000	8,700,000	2,000	14,000	9,323,000
	3	Carriers on Sea ...	*900,000	*20,274,000	*18,000	*42,000	*21,234,000
	4	Warehousemen ...	86,000	1,685,000	12,000	55,000	1,838,000
	5	Messengers, Telegraph	995,000	2,910,000	18,000	69,000	3,992,000
7	1	Agriculture, including small farmers	6,600,000	54,200,000	500,000	3,200,000	64,500,000
		Carried forward...	11,156,300	124,398,300	16,081,400	59,589,800	211,225,800

* Including Board and Lodging.

ESTIMATES OF THE EARNINGS

ESTIMATED AMOUNT OF EARNINGS—continued.

Order.		OCCUPATION.	MEN.		WOMEN.		TOTAL.
			Under 20 years.	20 to 65 years.	Under 20 years.	20 to 65 years.	
			£	£	£	£	£
		Brought forward...	11,156,300	124,398,300	16,081,400	59,589,800	211,225,800
8	1	Attending to Animals	147,000	2,493,000	...	2,000	2,642,000
9	1	Printers ...	682,000	3,594,000	45,000	32,000	4,353,000
		Lithographers	53,000	494,000	5,000	...	552,000
	2	Bookbinders	58,000	695,000	133,000	184,000	1,070,000
10	1	Engineers...	179,400	2,830,900	500	8,700	3,019,500
		Machinists	536,000	8,962,500	2,000	8,000	9,508,500
	2	Implement Makers	148,000	2,400,000	28,000	182,000	2,758,000
	3	Watchmakers	105,000	1,623,000	5,000	15,000	1,748,000
	4, 7	Scientific Instrument Makers ...	71,000	1,978,000	5,000	17,000	2,071,000
		Type Cutters	33,000	403,000	8,000	48,000	492,000
11	1	Builders ...	2,633,500	39,000,000	...	...	41,633,500
		Cabinet Makers, French Polishers	218,000	4,052,000	60,000	240,000	4,600,000
	3	Locksmiths, Gasfitters ..	90,000	1,574,000	...	...	1,664,000
		Wood Carvers and Gilders ...	83,000	1,189,000	69,000	148,000	1,489,000
12	12	Coachmakers, Saddlers ...	225,300	3,956,300	...	...	4,181,600
13	1	Shipwrights, &c. ...	*72,000	*2,397,000	...	...	*2,469,000
		Sailmakers	15,000	214,000	...	...	229,000
	3	Sugar Refinery, Mustard, &c. ...	13,000	227,000	3,000	24,000	267,000
14	3	Chemical Manufacture	19,000	917,000	19,000	26,000	981,000
15	1	Tobacco ...	598,000	38,000	102,000	171,000	909,000
16	2	Maltsters&Brewers' Cellarmen	72,000	2,361,000	2,000	16,000	2,451,000
		Milk Sellers	95,000	942,000	16,000	156,000	1,209,000
		Corn Millers	88,000	1,600,000	...	7,000	1,695,000
		Bakers and Confectioners	600,000	3,587,000	20,000	198,000	4,414,000
		Greengrocers	56,000	1,017,000	16,000	138,000	1,227,000
17	1	Woollen Manufacture	485,000	4,603,000	1,461,000	2,667,000	9,216,000
	2	Silk Manufacture	106,000	820,000	342,000	776,000	2,044,000
	3	Cotton Manufacture ...	1,697,700	11,620,200	5,813,900	9,428,000	28,559,800
	4	Flax, Linen, and Hemp ...	335,000	2,335,000	793,000	962,000	4,425,000
	5	Weavers, Dyers, Factory Hands	235,000	1,314,000	422,000	809,000	2,780,000
		Felt Carpet	68,000	602,000	153,000	344,000	1,167,000
18	1	Hosiery, Gloves, Buttons...	91,000	1,057,000	261,000	957,000	2,366,000
		Carried forward ...	21,094,200	235,294,200	25,874,800	77,153,500	359,416,700

* With allowance for the unemployed.

OF THE WORKING CLASSES.

ESTIMATED AMOUNT OF EARNINGS—*continued.*

Order.		OCCUPATION.	MEN.		WOMEN.		TOTAL.
			Under 20 years.	20 to 65 years.	Under 20 years.	20 to 65 years.	
			£	£	£	£	£
		Brought forward...	21,094,200	235,294,200	25,874,800	77,153,500	359,416,700
18	1	Hatters, Straw Hats ...	78,000	909,000	189,000	697,000	1,873,000
		Tailors, Milliners	721,000	5,924,000	3,097,000	14,013,000	23,755,000
		Shirt Manufacture	4,500	70,000	47,400	2,955,000	3,076,900
		Boots, Shoes, Patten Clogs ...	960,000	10,546,000	314,000	766,000	12,586,000
		Hair, Wig Makers	112,000	1,117,000	47,000	10,200	1,286,200
		Shawl Manufacture	...	110,000	6,000	18,000	134,000
		Umbrella Makers	15,000	166,500	36,000	87,000	304,500
19	1	Tallow, Soap, & Glue Manufacture ...	35,000	537,000	15,000	20,000	607,000
	2	Furriers, Tanners, &c.	153,000	2,738,000	93,000	244,000	3,228,000
	3	Hair Brush, &c. ...	44,000	430,000			474,000
20	1	Oil Millers ...	35,000	533,000	...	11,000	579,000
		Floor Cloth, Japanners, India Rubber, &c.	41,000	504,000	36,000	36,000	617,000
20	23	Willow, Cane, Timber Sawyers...	370,000	5,872,000	42,000	101,000	6,385,000
	4	Paper Manufacture, Envelopes, &c.	158,000	1,449,000	291,000	590,000	2,488,000
21	22	Miners	1,911,000	22,687,000	...	...	24,598,000
	2	Quarrymen ...	227,000	3,240,000	...	52,000	3,519,000
		Slate, Lime ...	39,000	759,000	...	...	798,000
		Brick and Tile ...	283,000	1,867,000	26,000	55,000	2,231,000
	3	Paviours and Platelayers	44,000	3,069,000			3,113,000
		Railway Labourers, Navvies ...	80,000	1,816,000	...	...	1,896,000
	4	Earthenware, Glass	144,000	2,602,000	221,000	350,000	3,317,000
	5,6	Salt and Waterworks	12,000	408,000	...	...	420,000
	7	Goldsmiths, Lapidaries	127,000	1,577,000	50,000	120,000	1,874,000
	8	Blacksmiths and Whitesmiths, Iron Manufacture, Nail, &c.	962,000	23,697,000	85,000	261,000	25,005,000
	9,12	Metal Manufacture	837,000	5,815,000	157,000	234,000	7,043,000
	1	Costermongers ...	79,000	794,000	39,000	735,000	1,647,000
	1	Refuse Matters ...	8,000	252,000	5,000	9,500	274,500
	2	General Labourers and Artisans ...	...	*28,000,000	...	*600,000	*28,600,000
			28,573,700	362,782,700	30,671,200	99,118,200	521,245,800

* With allowance for the unemployed.

(*Circular Letter.*)
WAGES AND EARNINGS OF THE LABOURING CLASSES.

5, Crown Office Row, Temple,
London, *June*, 1884.

Dear Sir,

Some years ago, at the instance of the late Mr. Bass, M.P., I collected some information on the Wages and Earnings of the Workpeople in the United Kingdom, which was most useful for my estimate of the total amount of income of the labouring classes. Having been asked by Sir Arthur Bass, M.P., to renew the inquiry, and to bring the information up to date, I venture to ask of your kindness the following questions:—

1. What are the present rates of wages in your industry?
2. When the workers are paid by time—viz., by the week, day, or hour—what are the rates paid to men, women, and children respectively? At what age adult wages begin?
3. If the workers are paid by piecework, could you give, from the Wagebook or otherwise, the average earnings of each class of workers for the last six months or for one year?
4. If the wages and earnings of workers in the different branches of work differ materially, what proportion receive the respective amounts—separating foremen, artisans, and labourers, and in all cases adding the amount paid for *overtime*?
5. Does the artisan pay any labourer or assistant out of his own wages? If so, how much?
6. How many hours per day and in the week the workers are expected to work?
7. If they enjoy other advantages in food, dress, or house accommodation besides their money wages, please state what such advantages are.
8. Are tools or implements supplied, or do they belong to the workpeople?

9. For how many weeks in the year the labourers can, generally, count on their work and wages? This I require in order to arrive at the annual income of the workers and their families.

10. Could you favour me with the fluctuations of wages in your industry for any period?

Your kind answers to all, or any of the above questions, will be considered and kept *quite private*, if so desired, the object of the inquiry being very general, not in the interest of any class, nor to serve any political or party purpose whatsoever, but simply to ascertain the facts as they are. With many thanks, and apologising for the trouble,

Believe me,

Dear Sir,

Yours faithfully,

LEONE LEVI,

Professor of the Principles of Commerce in King's College, London.

Chapter II.

ECONOMIC CONDITION OF THE WORKING CLASSES IN 1884 AND 1857.*

1. *Inquiries into the condition of the Working Classes.*

IT may seem ungenerous, if not officious, from time to time to inquire into the social condition of the labouring classes. Why are not similar inquiries instituted into the condition of other classes of society? Cogent reasons, however, justify a special solicitude for the welfare of the labouring classes. Their economic condition reflects the state of agriculture, commerce, and industry; their claim to share in a higher degree in the products of labour touches some of the most difficult problems of economic science; their virtues and vices illustrate in the closest manner the state and progress of civilisation and morals; and their number, some seventy per cent. of the entire population, gives them a weight and an influence in social and political questions which no politician can ignore or neglect. Who can, moreover, be callous to the penury and hardships of the less favoured among their number—the wretched victims often of disease and want? A stoic indifference to their sufferings is perilous. Nay, it deprives ourselves of the luxury of sympathy, even if it be out of our power to provide any substantial remedy.

> What though in scaly armour dressed,
> Indifference may repel
> The shafts of woe, in such a breast
> No joy can ever dwell.
>
> 'Tis woven in the world's great plan,
> And fixed by Heaven's decree,
> That all the true delights of man
> Should spring from sympathy.

Nor is it a question of sentiment. If sociology is to rise to a science, it must be by the careful observation and collection of facts recording the movement and evolution of different classes of the people. The deductive system of reasoning will not

---

* Substance of a Paper read at the Social Science Association Meeting in Birmingham, 1884, that being the twenty-seventh year since the first meeting held there.

help us much. It is from experience to law, and not from law to experience, that we must proceed. Twenty-seven years are but a short chapter in the history of society, nevertheless, let us treasure their teaching, for they cannot fail to help us in the elaboration of theories of wide application.

2. *Gradations among the Working Classes.*

Seventy per cent. of the population make the working classes (erroneously so-called *par excellence*, for I imagine brain workers have often a harder task than those engaged in manual labour) reach the total of some twenty-five millions. But they comprise many scarcely distinguishable from the middle classes. They embrace artisans and skilled workers, enamellers and lapidaries, machinists and engineers, with eyes and hands as cultivated as those of any other portion of the population, and as far removed from common labourers and miners as clerks and curates are from those who have reached the highest places in the liberal professions or wealthy merchants and bankers, all of whom pass under the category of the middle classes. In truth, during the last quarter of a century the higher branches of industry have greatly advanced; science and art have taken a deeper root, and the higher strata of the labouring classes have exercised an elevating influence over every branch of British labour. On the other hand, a very large number of the working classes are still low and degraded, ignorant and miserable. In describing the social or moral condition of any class of society, in the same manner as in depicting the state of any nation, we are apt to be swayed by the impressions produced by those who come more visibly before us, or by our own sanguine or depressed temperament, or by any fortuitous event which may happen to cross our path. But opinions thus formed and advanced, though true in a limited sense, are often erroneous as a real indication of the condition of the class or nation as a whole. Where possible we must be guided only by the averages of great numbers, for though failing to represent the true condition of distinct persons, an average is always truer as to the broad characteristics of the class.

3. *Physical Condition of the Working Classes.*

There is no reliable evidence of the physique of the people at any distinct period. The Anthropometric Committee of the

British Association* recently made extensive observations respecting the height, weight, girth of chest, drawing power, and other particulars of the people in different parts of the country, which will afford a useful standard whereby to compare their future progress. But no such observations were made before, and loose opinions that the people are apparently smaller or taller now than they were are not reliable data to go by. There are indeed good reasons for believing that the physical condition of the labouring classes is better now than it ever was. If the food of the people is more artificial than it used to be, they certainly have more of it. If the dress is made of more flimsy material, more yards of cloth are employed. Bad as in some cases the dwellings of the labouring classes are, they are immensely better in the great majority of cases than they used to be. The rate of mortality is less. In England and Wales it was 21·8 per 1000 in 1857, and 19·6 per 1000 in 1882. Cases of longevity are more numerous. And, whatever injury to health may arise from the increasing migration from country to town, it is greatly counteracted by improved sanitary arrangements, by the action of the Factory Laws, by the persistent legislation, for the prevention, as far as possible, of diseases incident to many occupations, and for the prevention of accidents in factories, mines, and workshops, and also for the preservation of life at sea. Two evils are directly affecting the physical condition of the people generally in large towns. The first is density of population and overcrowding. The second intemperance. The revelations made by the "Bitter Cry of Outcast London" as to the crowding of the poor in wretched habitations have, with reason, produced considerable alarm. And well may we trust that the Royal Commission now inquiring into the subject may suggest measures calculated to abate or prevent this, the first source of degeneration. Intemperance, it is to be lamented, exists to a large extent; yet there are indications that it is somewhat on the decrease. In 1857, the consumption of spirits, British and foreign, was in the proportion of 1·03 gallon per head. In 1875 it had risen to 1·30. In 1883 it fell to 1·06. In 1857 the consumption

---

* The general results of the inquiry relating to adult persons of the ages from 23 to 50 years were as follows:—

	Average height, statute inches, without shoes.	Average weight including clothes lbs.	Ratio lbs. weight per inch of statute height.
England	67·36	155·0	2·301
Wales	66·66	158·3	2·375
Scotland	68·71	165·3	2·406
Ireland	67·90	154·1	2·270

See *Transactions of the British Association for the Advancement of Science*, 1882.

of malt was 1·58 bushel, which, at 18 gallons per bushel, gave 2·4 gallons per head. In 1876 it had risen to 2 bushels, or 36 gallons. And in 1883 the consumption of beer was 27·1 gallons per head. What is better still, however, is that sounder views obtain regarding the consumption of alcohol, whether in excess or moderation, while the greater vigilance of the police in bringing before the magistrates all persons found in a state of drunkenness in the public streets, indicates that society no longer suffers manners at one time regarded with perfect indifference. From all sides there are evidences that, though much remains to be done for the improvement of the physical condition of the people, the forces which favour their well-being have been greater than those which operated towards their detriment.

4. *Progress of Education among the Working Classes.*

With matters pertaining to the health of the body we may unite what pertains to the health of the mind. At no former period greater strides have been made in the elementary education of the people than during the last fourteen years. Previous to 1870 the Committee of Council on Education was striving, notwithstanding the most strenuous opposition by some of the most liberal minds in Manchester, Birmingham, and other places, to assist education by making some grants to the National and British School Societies; but under that system only a few districts, and those mainly consisting of middle class people, were really provided with schools. The working classes were in most cases left out of all educational superintendence. They were not considered as coming within the range of real educational requirements. At all events, they were beyond the reach of those who took an interest in education. It was only in 1870 that a national system was effectively introduced, which by compelling the establishment of schools in every district proportionate to population, and by making attendance at school, where possible, compulsory, brought education fairly within the reach of the working classes. And the result has been that, whereas in 1857 the average number of children in attendance in primary schools in Great Britain was 531,000, in 1883 it increased to 3,560,000. Fear has been expressed that as workmen become educated they will regard with aversion the lower kinds of employments. I have no such fears. Depend upon it, if ignorance is likely to be the mother of pride and idleness, education is certain to engender humility and industry.

The work that has to be done will be done, and not neglected. Nay, it will be done all the more cleverly, and all the more pleasantly, because the workman is educated. During the last twenty-seven years we have also seen the formation of the Kensington Museum, and with it the extension of science and art classes, the circulation of objects of art, drawings, &c., and the promotion of technical education in connection with every branch of industry, all exercising a most beneficial influence not only on the work but on the workers. If ever the labouring classes were a source of danger to the State, they cannot be so accounted at this moment. We are not politicians here, yet it is impossible to ignore the important fact that by the Reform Act of 1867 the political rights of workmen were greatly extended, not only to their benefit, but to the benefit of the State, and that the Franchise Bill, which has just passed the House of Commons with such unexampled unanimity, provided for the enfranchisement of two millions of householders in country districts, all parties recognising that the exercise of civil rights may be safely and confidently entrusted in the hands of the masses of the people, whether in town or country.

5. *Are our Working Men less Laborious?*

A common impression exists that our working men are less laborious and active than they were; that they work fewer hours, and that during those hours they put forth less energy, so that where two workmen were once sufficient to do a certain amount of work, three are now necessary. Doubtless the Factory Acts have reduced the number of hours of actual work in factories and workshops, and the influence of this legislation has extended to all branches of trade and industry. Early closing has also been everywhere in the ascendant, and for many years past Bank holidays and half-day holidays have given a taste for a little too much rest. Would that it were always used aright. Again, the extension of machinery has removed from the shoulders of our working men some of the harder tasks; and whether out of regard to health or as the natural influence of better wages, there is doubtless shown a decided aversion to all slavish and protracted labour. Yet with all this we have no statistical evidence that less work is being performed. On the contrary, in every branch of industry production has largely increased. As an illustration, take the following facts regarding minerals and shipping:—

		Production 1857	1882	Increase per cent.
Coal	tons	63,394,707	156,499,977	146
Pig iron	,,	3,659,064	8,586,680	134
Shipping built	,,	250,472	760,576	204
Cotton manufactures exported (piece goods) yrds.		1,979,270,780	4,538,888,500	129
Iron and steel exported	tons	1,532,386	4,043,309	163

No doubt this increase has been accomplished largely by an augmentation of steam power, and the extension and improvement of machinery and implements of all kinds; nevertheless human labour is as much wanted as ever, and, what is more, it is always amply available. Let us not grudge any increase of ease to our working classes. Only employers have a right to expect that what labour workmen give shall be given heartily and vigorously, and not in a stinted and perfunctory manner. A contract of labour for wages is essentially mutual, and should be performed loyally on both sides. Nor is it to be desired that the relations of master and men should be of a purely mercenary character. Many founders of our colossal houses look back to the days when masters and men were working for the common good, when each and all felt deep sympathy for the success of the work, and when each and all felt personal pride in its excellence, as the halcyon days of their prosperity.

6. *Relations of Employers and Employed.*

The relations of masters and men have in truth been much strained within the last twenty-seven years, and the conflicts between capital and labour have been keen and frequent in nearly every branch of industry. It is some time now since the illegality of combinations of labour was removed, yet it is not many years since Trade Unions were not allowed to have any status in a court of justice, because part of their funds was expended in the illegal act of restraining the industries of their members. This prohibition was taken away by the 34 & 35 Vict. c. 31, 1871. Again, it was only in 1867 that the Masters and Servants Act was passed, which put an end to the power of the master to pursue criminally a labourer for any breach of contract; a proceeding exceedingly harsh, all the more that it was only on the masters' side. By that Act jurisdiction in such cases was given to Magistrates; but by the Conspiracy and Protection of

Property Act, 38 & 39 Vict. c. 86, 1875, the same was transferred to the County Courts—another evidence of the desire of the Legislature to place all persons, whether employers or employed, under equal laws. Still more recently, in 1880, the Employers' Liability Act, 43 & 44 Vic. c. 42, was passed, by which the working classes succeeded in throwing upon the employers the responsibility for any personal injury caused in consequence of defects in the condition of the ways, works, machinery, or plant, or negligence of any person in the service of their employers, together with a right of compensation for the same. Reforms such as these commend themselves now as eminently equitable and just, and yet what difficulties and objections were urged against them! Seldom, how seldom, are grievances remedied with alacrity and generosity! Years generally pass ere they are admitted to exist, and then how slow is the administration of the necessary remedies!

7. *Comparison of Wages*, 1857 *and* 1884.

With the enormous increase of wealth in the United Kingdom, the position of the working classes has likewise greatly improved. In a large number of instances working men of 1857 have become middle-class men of 1884. Many a workman of that day has now a shop or an hotel, has money in the bank or shares in shipping or mills. Cases of rising from the ranks are by no means so rare as we might imagine. But working men of the present day are much better off than they were twenty-seven years ago, for all wages are higher. In 1857 the wages of common labourers were 15s. to 17s. a week; now they are from 20s. to 22s., showing an increase of 30 per cent. In 1857 a joiner got 27s.; now he gets 33s. 6d., or 36s., with piecework, showing an increase of 24 per cent. Agricultural wages have risen more than 30 per cent., from 8s. and 10s., to 13s. and 15s. and even 18s. a week. Domestic servants, formerly satisfied with £9 and £10 per annum, now easily get £14 and £16. Seamen's wages have risen from 50s. to 80s. per month. But even these wages fail to give a full view of the improved condition of the labouring classes, for wherever piecework obtains, the wages average about one-eighth above day work, whilst all overtime is paid at varying rates. And we must add to this the fact that in many industries women are able to earn good wages, and children's labour is much required. Taking a comprehensive view of the entire range of industries, bearing in mind the actual rise in the rates of wages, the increasing amount of piecework and overtime, the improved earnings of women and children, and the receipt here and there from interest of money from investments, or from rent of house saved, equal to fresh income, I think I am justified in assuming that the working classes, as a whole, are in receipt of 30 per cent. more in 1884 than they were receiving in 1857, or, in other words, that if the total weekly receipt of a family from all sources in 1857 amounted to 24s., now they reach at least 32s. a week.

8. *Expenditure of the Working Classes.*

But are our working classes, with their larger amount of income, better or worse off than they were twenty-seven years ago? Are their present wages sufficient for their necessary expenses? The answer to these questions must depend, first, on the particular class of workmen, such as artisans or labourers, town or country people, to which they refer; second, on the purchasing power of the sovereign,* and third, on the habits and manners of certain families, especially as regards economy or waste, temperance or intemperance, &c. It is impossible, in a general survey like this, to consider the case of each class separately, and we must be satisfied with certain general characteristics. Take the item of house rent; it is considerably dearer than it was in London, Birmingham, and other large places; but domestic servants know nothing of it. In small towns, in agricultural districts, and in fishing villages, scarcely any rise has taken place. The Rev. Charles Joseph, in his evidence before the Artisans' Dwelling Inquiry Committee, in the borough of Birmingham, in June last, gave some interesting facts on the relation of wages to house rent in Birmingham, respecting twenty families—father, mother, and an average of 3·5 children each. Their average wages amounted to 27s. 6d. weekly (exclusive of all other sources of income), and they paid on an average 6s. a week of rent, or in the proportion of 23·7 per cent., but the proportion varied from 15·6 to 33·3 per cent. of the wages. It appears, moreover, that sober men paid 40 per cent. more rent; and were in that degree better housed than drunken men, the average of the sober men, giving 33s. 4d. wages and 5s. rent, and of drunken men 31s. 8d. wages, and 3s. rent. And these facts respecting house rent may be taken to represent the case of most of our large towns. Yet the average relation of rental to income for the whole country cannot be

* See purchase power of the sovereign in Appendix.

taken as approaching these figures. Taking the total income of the British people at £1,000,000,000, and the total annual value of house property at £100,000,000, the proportion is 10 per cent. With house rent we should put fire, light, and local rates. Coal and gas are now both cheaper than they were twenty-seven years ago; and as for rates, they are seldom paid by the working classes, at least in a direct manner, for the higher rents of rooms include of course all rates paid by the tenants of the entire houses. In calculating the cost of food, the important fact must be borne in mind that if, on the one hand, the greater number of articles of food are cheaper now than they were, on the other their consumption is considerably greater. Sugar, tea, rice are cheaper; meat, butter, and cheese are dearer. Comparing the consumption of articles of food imported per head of the entire population, and their prices as given in the Statistical Abstract for 1871 and 1883, we have the following facts:—

	Consumption.			Prices.			
	1871. lbs.	1883. lbs.	Increase per cent.	1871. Per cwt.	1883. Per cwt.	Increase per cent.	Decrease per cent.
Bacon and Hams	3·38	10·96	103	s. 49·20	53·08	7	—
Butter	4·69	7·18	51	l. 5·20	5·01	—	8
Cheese	4·25	5·51	30	l. 2·75	2·72	—	1
Sugar (raw)	41·51	61·87	49	s. 25·10	20·10	—	19
Sugar (refined)	5·29	9·87	89	s. 36·15	27·22	—	24
Tea	3·92	4·80	22	d. 16·44 lb.	12·46 lb.	—	26
Rice	7·47	12·43	66	s. 10·19	8·20	—	19

If the people consumed in 1883 60 per cent. more of these commodities than they did in 1871, whilst their prices have decreased less than 15 per cent., where is the economy from their cheapness?

The consumption of alcoholic drink we have already seen to be nearly the same now as in 1857, but the consumption of non-alcoholic drinks has largely increased. Lime-juice cordials, ginger-beer, lemonade, &c., constitute now important articles of consumption. And the consumption of milk has also increased. Would, indeed, that this most valuable article of diet for adults and children alike were more abundant and purer, both from water and deleterious substances! There are no means of estimating the quantities of articles of clothing used, but their prices are considerably lower, as will be seen from the following average prices given in the Statistical Abstract for the last fifteen years, just published.

		1869.	1883.	Per cent. reduction.
Cotton piece goods (plain)	... per yard d.	3·79	d. 2·61	31
,, ,, (printed)	... ,,	,, 4·91	,, 3·62	26
,, ,, (mixed materials)	,,	,, 9·68	,, 5·81	39
Woollen stuffs	,,	,, 14·52	,, 9·94	31
,, flannels, &c.	... ,,	,, 17·68	,, 14·82	16
Boots and shoes	per doz. pairs s.	60·82	s. 60·10	1

There are, however, other items besides food, drink, and clothing which must be considered. At one time our artisans and town labourers were generally living within reach of their factories and workshops. Now they are often compelled to live at two or three miles distance, and so the cost of travelling by tramways or railways has become a necessary expenditure. At one time the greater number of workmen never disturbed themselves with the education of their children. Now they are bound to send their children to school and pay for the same. Many workmen now subscribe to a trade union or friendly society who had no such expense before. And, with the greater number of holidays, the call for an excursion to the country seems natural, involving, of course, considerable expense. It is difficult, as already stated, to compare the actual cost of living now and twenty-seven years ago, and still more to estimate how the altered circumstances affect the special position of different classes of workmen. The agricultural labourer, with a cottage for £2 a year, and a piece of land giving him vegetables in abundance, and the facility for keeping a pig, is very differently situated from a town labourer paying 6s. a week for rent and having to buy everything. A workman in a provincial town has much less expense than one in London. The position of a man with a large family and that of a single man cannot be compared; nor that of one with a family all grown up, and several of them earning something, and of one with a family all small and at school. Above all, a workman who drinks, smokes, and wastes his money in gambling is, of course, very much worse off than one who has no such vices. Still, as a test of the altered cost of living now and twenty-seven years ago, I venture on an ideal budget of a working man's family, living in a large town, and earning respectively 24s. a week in 1857 and 32s. in 1884. I have taken no account of any extravagance, but simply put down what may be considered reasonable or necessary, at least with present notion of things, and the results are as follows:—

Workman's Budget.

1857.

Receipts.		£ s. d.	Expenditure.	£ s. d.
Fifty weeks' wages at 24s. per week, exclusive of other income		60 0 0	Bread, 28 lbs. per week, at 7d. per quartern	10 12 0
Deficiency		3 2 8	Meat, 4 lbs. per week, at 8d. per lb.	6 18 8
			Butter, 1 lb. per week, at 1s. 2d. per lb.	3 0 0
			Cheese, ½ lb. per week, at 9d. per lb.	0 19 0
			Sugar, 3 lbs. per week, at 5d. per lb.	3 5 0
			Tea, ¼ lb per week, at 4s. per lb.	5 4 0
			Vegetables and potatoes	2 0 0
			Milk	1 0 0
			Eggs	5 4 0
			*Drink, at 2s. a week	2 10 0
			Coal and gas	2 10 0
			House rent, at 4s. per week	10 0 0
			*Tobacco, at 1s.	2 10 0
			Clothing	4 0 0
			Furniture	1 0 0
			Travelling and amusements	1 0 0
			Sundries — church, doctor, &c.	2 0 0
		£63 2 8		£63 2 8

1884.

Receipts.	£ s. d.	Expenditure.	£ s. d.
Fifty weeks' wages at 32s. per week, exclusive of other income	80 0 0	Bread, 28 lbs. per week, at 6d. per quartern	9 2 0
		Meat, 5 lbs. per week, at 10d. per lb.	10 16 0
		Butter, 1 lb. per week, at 1s. 6d. per lb.	5 17 0
		Cheese, ½ lb. per week, at 10d. per lb.	1 2 0
		Sugar, 3 lbs. per week, at 3d. per lb.	1 19 0
		Tea, ¼ lb. per week, at 2s. 8d. per lb.	3 9 0
		Vegetables and potatoes	2 0 0
		Milk	2 10 0
		Eggs	1 10 0
		*Drink, at 2s. a week	6 4 0
		Coal and gas	2 0 0
		House rent, at 6s. per week	15 12 0
		*Tobacco, at 1s.	2 10 0
		Clothing	4 0 0
		Furniture	1 0 0
		Travelling and amusements	3 0 0
		Sundries — church, doctor, education, &c.	2 10 0
			£74 1 0
		Surplus	5 19 0
	£80 0 0		£80 0 0

* The expenditure for alcoholic drink and tobacco, though assumed, must not be considered as necessary, for it is at most a simple luxury, all the less justifiable where the wages are low.

If I am right in this estimate, it will be seen—First, that the proportion of expenditure in the two periods was as follows:—

	1857. Per cent.	1884. Per cent.
Food and drink	65·57	61·97
House rent, fire, and light	20·47	24·78
Other expenses	13·96	13·25
	100·00	100·00

so that what is gained in the cost of food goes mostly in additional house rent. Second, that, whilst in 1857 such a family could not make the two ends meet, in 1884 they may have a surplus of £8 9s., and if in the interval the family have given up the use of alcoholic drinks and tobacco, their surplus will amount to about £16 a year. But this is, after all, an ideal budget. In truth the whole question whether, under any circumstance, a family with a large or small income is likely to be rich or poor, happy or unhappy, depends on good or bad management and household economy, on well-sustained thrift, or on waste and extravagance. Well might Robert Burns, in one of his letters, say:—

"O frugality! thou mother of ten thousand blessings. Thou cook of fat beef and dainty greens, thou manufacturer of warm Shetland hose and comfortable surtouts! Thou old housewife darning the decayed stockings with thy ancient spectacles on thy aged nose! Lead me where the sunny exposure of plenty and the hot walks of profusion produce those useful fruits of luxury, exotics in this world and natives of paradise."

9. *Moral Effects of High and Low Wages.*

It has been alleged that high wages only lead to extravagance and folly: for my part I see no reason for such a proposition. As a rule, and in the long run, scarcity, low wages, and scantiness of food, go hand in hand with high mortality, drunkenness and crime; while abundance, high wages, and full consumption, go hand in hand with low mortality, temperance, and good behaviour. The relation between times of scarcity and dear bread and crime and insurrection has often been observed; dear bread and cheap bread being taken as the symbols of scarcity and abundance. But high or low wages are a better standard by which to measure the condition of the people than the value of bread, inasmuch as they command more or less of all the comforts of life. Let an illustration pregnant with lessons suffice. In the five years, from 1857 to 1861, the total amount of imports and exports to and from the United Kingdom averaged £12 1s. 0d. per head of the population, and the number of offences against the person and property in England and Wales was in the proportion of 7647 per 1,000,000 persons, or in the relation of thirty-one offences to every shilling of trade. In 1882, when the trade of the United Kingdom increased to £20 7s. 10d. per head of the population, the number of such offences diminished to 6566 per million, giving a proportion of sixteen offences for every shilling of trade. In 1862-66, years of the great cotton famine, the number of persons committed for trial in Lancashire was in the proportion of 1·34 per 1000. In 1872-76, years of great prosperity, the proportion of committals was 0.98 per 1000. And were not the recent dreadful agrarian outrages in Ireland to a large extent the direct results of successive bad harvests? A sudden increase of wages, as in the colliery districts in 1872-73, may find the recipients utterly unprepared for their good fortune. And so we have heard of miners indulging in Champagne wine, and of puddlers purchasing for themselves sealskin waistcoats. But reason speedily asserts her higher sway. The housewife eagerly arrests a portion of the higher wages to furnish the bare rooms, to fill the empty cupboard, and to clothe the children. Little by little, as the novel condition with its bountiful stores is realised, self-respect increases, sobriety of conduct is induced, and the family as a whole rises to habits of virtue and propriety.

10. *The Law of Wages and Profit Sharing.*

The hard lines laid down by political economists, that the rates of wages must depend on the supply and demand of labour, and on the amount which the employer can afford to give in the shape of wages, are complained of and protested against by some of our working men, and the theory has been propounded that workmen ought to participate in a more direct manner in the produce of their own labour, be it by the master agreeing to give them a percentage of their profits over and above their wages, or by the workmen becoming themselves masters by means of co-operative companies for production. The concession in some cases of a percentage of the profits of labour in addition to the ordinary wages would doubtless give a great incentive to industry and improvement. I doubt, however, whether profit sharing could be made general or obligatory. If the workman is to acquire a right to a participation of the profits and loss, and consequently a right to an account, practically he would become a partner; but can we expect masters to take all their men into partnership, and to bind themselves to the publication of their affairs to the extent involved? If the workman is to be entitled to a share of the profits, would he not have to bear his share of any loss? This seems, indeed, involved in the principle of arranging the rate of wages by reference to the profits of the master. In any case such a system could at most apply to foremen or permanent workmen, and never to the great body of workers who constantly migrate from place to place. Co-operative companies for production have in many cases succeeded well, but in many other cases the results have been very disappointing. The difficulties, I apprehend, are the want of able and trustworthy men to manage the work profitably, the danger of loss which workman can ill sustain, and the want of capital great enough to carry on operations on a large scale, the only mode of securing economy so indispensable for profitable investments. It is, however, proposed to convene an industrial remuneration conference at the commencement of next year, to consider these questions with a view to ascertain by what means the labouring classes may more fully share in the products of industry, and, as a member of the committee nominated by the Statistical Society for the conduct of that conference, I earnestly trust it may help us to the right determination of the difficult problems of economic science involved in the relation of capital and labour.*

* The following are some of the points which will be brought forward for discussion at the Conference:—
1. The existing system by which the products of industry are distributed.
2. Do any artificial and remediable causes influence prejudicially
  (a) the stability of industrial employment?
  (b) the steadiness of rates of wages?
  (c) the well-being of the working classes?
3. How far, in what manner, and by what means would the more general distribution of capital contribute, or not contribute, to
  (a) an increase in the products of industry?
  (b) the well-being of the classes dependent upon the use of capital?
  (Co-operative production, profit-sharing, &c.)
4. How far, in what manner, and by what means, would a more general ownership of land (peasant proprietorship), or of an interest in land (tenant right), conduce, or not conduce, to
  (a) the increased production of wealth?
  (b) the welfare of the classes affected by the change?
5. Does existing legislation, or the incidence of existing legislation, affect prejudicially
  (a) the production of industrial wealth?
  (b) the well-being of the classes engaged in the production?
  (c) the natural or the most beneficial distribution of the accumulating products of national industry? (including succession duties, friendly societies, insurance, &c.)
Can any of these be promoted by changes in existing legislation or taxation? (See a Digest of the Conference on p. 40.)

11. *Investments of the Working Classes.*

The real and best hope of the labouring classes must ever depend on the skilful administration of their earnings, and on the right investment of their savings; and what has been accomplished in this direction may be gathered from the following facts. In 1857, the capital of the Trustees Savings Banks amounted to £35,000,000. In 1883, the capital of the Trustees and Post Office Savings Banks combined amounted to £86,756,000. But besides this, in 1883, the Building Societies had £47,000,000 and the Friendly and Industrial Societies £20,600,000; making a total of about £154,000,000, of which one-third at least may be taken to belong to the working classes. Nor is this all, for the Yorkshire Penny Bank had in 1883 as much as £1,596,000 to the credit of its depositors, while not a few of the labouring classes have shares in ships and mills, and houses of their own, besides their interest in building societies, to say nothing of the property invested in the furniture of the homes of the working classes, many of them being remarkable for comfort and neatness. In the investment of small savings the chief considerations must ever be safety, availableness, and increase: safety, for what has been set aside by hard sacrifices and careful economies must not be lightly hazarded; availableness, for the working man moves from place, and may some day emigrate to the Far West or the Antipodes. Increase I have put third in order; still it must be sought, so that it may assist in however small a manner the wants of a family. Money deposited in the Savings Banks is safe and available at any time. The Friendly Societies, with their provisions for sickness, old age, and burial, must ever be useful and popular, though care should be taken in the selection of the particular society, for many of them are in an unsound position. And Building Societies, whether with a view to building a house for oneself or for investment, are likewise attractive. Where the workman is well settled in a locality and can afford it, the purchase of a house may well engage his earliest sympathy.

12. *Prospects of the Working Classes.*

It is time, however, for me to draw these observations to a close. Taken as a whole, the working classes of the United Kingdom may be said to be stronger in physique, better educated, with more time at their command, in the enjoyment of greater political rights, in a more healthful relation towards their employers, receiving higher wages, and better able to effect some savings in 1884, than they were in 1857; and if they are not satisfied with remaining at home on these conditions, their field of labour is wider than ever, emigration agents making the most tempting offers for their transport to the land of promise. I am not given to indulge in fancies or poetry. I prefer, with Swift,

> Leaving the wits the spacious air,
> With license to build castles there.

And I must remember that, " if the young dreamer glowering in the fire, laughing at the gusty flame, builds castles in the air, older eyes than his are dazzled by a glare, hearts are broken, and heads are turned with castles in the air." There is not much danger, however, in predicting that the future of the working classes is likely to be brighter than the past. It is something to say, that the era of servitude and ignorance, and the era of monopoly and privilege are past and for ever. But it is satisfactory to think that educated labour is likely to be in greater and greater request. Desponding minds see in any temporary diminution of trade and manufacture a sign of decadence and eventual relapse of British industry. I have no such fear. The world was never so open as it is now, despite the exclusive tariffs which improvident Governments have enacted, and the thousand millions and more of persons inhabiting it have scarcely realised the wealth that lies under their feet, and the vast benefits arising from intercommunion and commerce. The *rôle* of England may not be to provide France, or Italy, Germany or the United States, with merchandise which they can produce better for themselves. But by keeping pace with the advance of industry, she will be always able to supply the millions of the human race with products of universal utility, while, with the wide ocean ever open to her seamen, she will for the future as in the past be the trafficker of the earth, the carrier of the world. Nor will British workmen linger behind if, rising to a level with their opportunities and privileges, they will secure for themselves a position suited to their rights and aspirations.

Methinks I see, at no great distance of time, the great volume of the labouring classes slowly, yet surely, by improvement and by emigration, yield to softer influences, waste and intemperance rebuked and vanquished, the wretched hovel and polluted atmosphere no longer sapping the strength and morals of the people. Methinks I see the British labourer in the enjoyment of a fair share of material comfort and intellectual culture, with manners more refined and morals more elevated, leading a laborious and dignified life; and in all public questions exercising an appreciable and wholesome influence.

DIGEST OF PROCEEDINGS OF THE INDUSTRIAL REMUNERATION CONFERENCE.

THE Conference was held on the 28th, 29th, and 30th January, under the presidency of the Right Honble. Sir Charles Dilke, M.P., and its proceedings indicate the opinions now held by some of the most intelligent among the working men and capitalists of the country upon the various questions considered in the report.

FIRST QUESTION.

" Has the increase of the products of industry within the last 100 years tended most to the benefit of capitalists and employers, or to that of the working classes, whether artisans, labourers or others, and in what proportion in any given period ? "

Sir Thomas Brassey gave facts tending to show that progress—real progress—has been made towards a more satisfactory social order, though we are very far from having attained to an ideal state of perfection. Mr. Lloyd Jones adverted to the discrepancy in the statements made of the total income of the working classes by different statisticians, and gave as his opinion that the working people are not progressing in comfort and independence commensurate with the increase of the nation in productive powers, nor with the actual growth of wealth. Mr. D. Cunningham in a paper on the rate of wages paid by the Dundee Harbour Trustees during the last 25 years, showed that the wages of workmen generally had increased from 60 to 80 per cent. in the period named, while the cost of the necessaries of life remained, one thing with another, much the same as before.

Miss Simcox contended that the chief benefit of the industrial progress of the last century has been reaped among capitalists by the greatest capitalists, among employers of labour by the largest employers; in general, by the dealers in commodities (labour included) rather than by makers or producers; and among makers and producers by those engaged in the most skilled rather than the most laborious work. Mr. W. Saunders gave particulars of the condition of the agricultural labourers in a district of Wiltshire where the wages are very low.

Mr. Lowthian Bell read a paper on the existing mode of distribution of the products of industry in the chemical works, collieries, ironstone mines, and blast furnaces in the North-east of England. He stated that during the last 25 years the wages paid in the chemical works increased $37\frac{1}{2}$ per cent., while during the same period the average value of the products declined to the extent of 40 per cent. On the Tyne 13 establishments have been broken up and sold as old material, accompanied by a reduction of 24 per cent. in the quantity of soda produced on its banks. The wealth and luxury of the capitalists are sometimes estimated on a wrong basis when contrasting them with the earnings of his workmen. "If," he said, "we were informed that the average earnings of all the people engaged in working the minerals, and smelting pig iron therefrom, were 4s. per day, and that the proprietor of the mines and furnaces received £25,000 a year as his share of the profits, it might be supposed by many that here was manifestly an unequal division of the accumulated wealth of this country. In order to earn his £25,000, however, something like £15,000 ought to be set aside to meet the interest on the capital expended on the mines and furnaces. Out of the balance of £10,000 which falls to the share of the smelter have to be paid depreciation of his money, the cost of which must be returned by the time the minerals are exhausted, interest on his working capital, and profit for carrying on the business. It would further appear that the sum of £10,000 belonging to the capitalist only represents 7·14 per cent. (1s. 5d. in the pound) on the wages paid for labour, so that an increase to this extent to the workman's earnings would sweep away his profits, properly so called, as well as the depreciation fund, and a further addition of 10·71 per cent. to the workman's pay, would leave the owner of the establishment without a penny to meet any of the charges enumerated as coming against it. In this estimate it has been assumed that £10,000 a year would be enough to afford a profit to the smelter, and to form a sinking fund to redeem the capital expended in sinking the pits, &c. In many cases, however, nearly the whole of the £10,000 might be absorbed for the latter purpose alone.

Second Question.

"Do any remedial causes influence prejudicially the continuity of industrial employment, the rate of wages, and the well-being of the working classes?"

Mr. W. Owen, of the Potteries, urged that, as combination of the units of labour is a necessity if working men are to possess equality in bargaining with employers, unionism should be fostered by the class. The trades that are disorganised often obtain less than the market value of their labour through not unitedly asserting their claim to it. By the completion and extension of unionism, many of the prejudicial influences upon work and wages could be removed, and a great step taken toward the perfect unity of capital and labour, in the form of productive and distributive co-operation.

Mr. J. Maudslay, of the Operative Cotton Spinners, urged that the system under which the workman stands alone and offers his services to the highest bidder, tested by results, has proved a complete failure.

Professor Marshall proposed no remedies for discontinuity of employment, save those which threw no great new responsibility on the state, and were, at all events, harmless. Among these he instanced greater temperance in changes of fashion, and want of increasing economic knowledge.

Professor Beesley, on behalf of the Positivist Society, urged that the principal cause influencing prejudicially the continuity of industrial employment, the rate of wages, and the well-being of the working classes, is the prevalence of wrong theories as to the organization of the industrial class, and the duties incumbent on its members. What is wanted is not a transference of capital from one set of persons to another, but that those who possess it should use it well. No serious improvement will take place until public opinion treats the wealth of the capitalist as a fund entrusted to him by society, to be administered for the benefit of society, and more especially of that particular group of workers for which he is responsible.

Mr. W. J. Harris, M.P., argued that the opening of our ports to the free introduction of manufactured goods, and even of half manufactured goods, has been of great disadvantage to the wage earning class, and advocated the imposition of import duties as a remedy.

Mr. W. H. Houldsworth, M.P., said that since industry is governed by the law of supply and demand it was scarcely possible to have any stability of industrial employment, or steadiness in the rates of wages.

Mr. Sedley-Taylor, M.A., read a paper in favour of profit sharing between employers and employed. The fact that under the existing system of remunerating labour the amount of a workman's earnings stand in no direct relation to the prosperity of the concern which employs him, is a cause influencing prejudicially the welfare of the working classes.

Mr. B. Jones said that there are two great causes detrimental to the working classes' well-being—viz., insufficient income, and inefficient expenditure.

Third Question.

"Would the more general distribution of capital or land, or the State management of capital or land, promote or impair the production of wealth, and the welfare of the community?"

Valuable papers were read on the subject by Mr. A. Balfour, on land reformers and the nation; H. R. Wallace, LL.D., on how to cause wealth to be more equally divided; Professor Newnan, on behalf of the Land Nationalization Society; Lord Bramwell, and Mr. Frederic Harrison; but they enter on matters beyond the scope of the present work.

Chapter III.
RECENT CHANGES IN THE DISTRIBUTION OF WEALTH.*

1. *Value of Estimates of National Income and National Wealth.*

MANY attempts have been made to arrive at the annual income of the people of the United Kingdom; not, indeed, from any sentiment of vanity or sheer curiosity, but to obtain the necessary data for the appreciation of many economic and social problems of the greatest practical importance. But the problem is difficult to solve, because many branches of income defy any valuation, because different branches of income have not the same value, because such values are subject to constant fluctuations; and because, when we have estimated the income of the different classes of the people, their aggregate will not represent the income of the nation as a whole; the income of one section, as in the case of the professional classes—the domestic service, &c.—being, in reality, the expenditure of another section. All attempts, moreover, to estimate the income of the nation can only be of an approximate character. Enough, indeed, if we can come within a measurable distance of the real truth.

2. *Estimated Amounts of Income and Wealth.*

As far back as in the reign of Henry VIII. a general survey was made of the kingdom, including the number of its inhabitants, their ages, professions, wealth, and other particulars, when the entire income was estimated at £4,000,000 † per annum; which, with a population of about 5,000,000, gave a proportion of 16s. per head. In 1822 Lord Liverpool valued the income of Great Britain at £250,000,000; which, with a population of 14,400,000, gave a proportion of £17 per head. In 1854 Mr. M'Culloch ‡ estimated the income at £370,000,000; which, with a population of 21,600,000, gave a proportion of £17 per head. None of these estimates, however, evidently included the

---

* A Paper read at the British Association for the Advancement of Science, held at Southport, 1883.
† Dr. Colquhoun, *Wealth, Power, and Resources of the British Empire*, p. 148, 1815.
‡ M'Culloch, *Account of the British Empire*, vol. ii., p. 526.

incomes of the labouring classes. Of such income there was but little knowledge till 1866, when I began to inquire into, and unite together, their wages and earnings, and found them amounting to upwards of £400,000,000 per annum. In 1868 Mr. Dudley Baxter gave his valuable paper on national income; and he estimated the total amount for the United Kingdom at £814,000,000; which, on a population of 30,000,000, gave a proportion of £20 17s. per head. And in 1881, the population being about 35,000,000, the income has been estimated at £1,000,000,000 per annum, or £28 per head. In a similar manner calculations have been made of the capital of the State. Gregory King in 1688 * estimated the total value of England at £650,000,000. Dr. Becke in 1798 estimated the capital at £995,000,000; and in the same year Mr. Pitt estimated it at £1,125,000,000. In 1812 Dr. Colquhoun † estimated the capital value of the United Kingdom at £2,700,000,000. In 1842 Mr. Porter ‡ estimated the amount of personal property at £2,200,000,000, and of real property £2,382,000,000; total, £4,582,000,000. And in 1878 Mr. Giffen estimated it at £8,500,000,000. §

---

* *Natural and Political Observations upon the State and Condition of England,* 1696.

† See Dr. Colquhoun's work, p. 55.

‡ *Progress of the Nation.*

§ Estimates of a like character have also been made in France, Germany, Austria, and the United States of America:—
Germany and Austria.—Neumann-Spällart, *Uebersichten über Produktion, Verkehr und Handel in der Weltwirthschaft,* 1878; Michaelis, *Die Gliederung der Gesellschaft nach dem Wohlstande,* Leipzig, 1878; Soetbeer, *Umfang und Vertheilung des Volks-Einkommens in Preussischen Staate,* Leipzig, 1879.
France.—Vauban, *Projet d'une dîme royale,* Paris (Guillaumin), 1843. Vol i. of the *Economiste financier du XVIII. siècle;* Lavoisier, *De la richesse territoriale de la France,* Paris (Guillaumin), 1847. *Mélange d'économie politique* (by E. Daire and G. De Molinari); Lagrange, *Essai d'arithmétique politique sur les premiers besoins de l'intérieur de la République* (ibid.); Block, *Statistique de la France,* Paris, 1878; *Dictionnaire de la politique.* 2de éd. Paris, 1875, art. ' France ;' Mony, *Etude sur le travail,* Paris, 1877; Vacher, ' La fortune nationale de la France,' *Journal de la Société de Statistique de Paris,* Nov. 1878; De Foville, ' De quelques évaluations récentes du capital national,' *Economiste français,* December 28, 1878, and January 28, 1879.
England.—Porter, *On the Progress of the Nation,* London, 1847; Capps, *The National Debt Financially Considered,* London, 1859; Levi, *On Taxation,* London, 1860; Dudley Baxter, *National Debt,* 1871. *National Income,* 1868; Giffen, ' Recent Accumulation of Capital in the United Kingdom,' *Journal of the Statistical Society,* March, 1878; Newmarch, *On the Progress of the Foreign Trade of the United Kingdom since* 1856; June, 1878.
Essai sur la question d'une statistique de revenu national (Commission permanente du Congrès International de Statistique), Mémoire, 1876.
Annali di Statistica, vol. 15, 1880. "Proposal of Professor Salandra of a Calculation of National Wealth in Italy."

But these varied estimates are not strictly comparable, however useful they may be as recording the results arrived at at different times by earnest and *bonâ fide* labourers in statistical science. We do not know the method pursued by each, or whether the income of every class of the community has been duly computed in each case. If we compare the income of the people of the United Kingdom at the extreme periods embraced, making allowance for the altered value of money and the difference in the purchasing power, the economic progress, however large, thereby indicated, may easily be accounted for. But if we compare each estimate with the preceding one, the results present some decided anomalies. Recent estimates have certainly the advantage of the income-tax assessments, which represent the amount for which the persons subject to the tax are willing to be rated. And though there may be in many cases the temptation to under-estimate that income so as to escape the tax in all or in part, still, on the aggregate, the range of error is considerably less by this method than by other modes of valuation.

3. *Changes in the Distribution of Wealth.*

The purpose of this paper, however, is not to examine critically the estimates already made of the income of the people of the United Kingdom, nor to offer any exhaustive estimate of my own. What I aim at is to elicit from the materials now at hand some indication of the recent changes in the distribution of property, more especially in relation to the estimated income of the labouring classes. Within the last thirty years great changes have taken place in the economic condition of the people. The introduction of free trade—or, more correctly stated, a more economic financial and commercial policy—the great extension of railways, the discoveries of gold in California and Australia, the enjoyment of a lengthened period of comparative peace, and the development of resources in the British colonies and dependencies, have each and all had surprising effects on the trade and industries of the realm. Have the higher, middle, and labouring classes participated in the same proportion in the increasing wealth of the nation.

4. *Classification of the Population.*

It is difficult to classify the population under any well defined categories. Generally, we have the broad distinction between income taxpayers and non-income taxpayers. But the number of income taxpayers at any time is affected by the changes made in the limit of incomes subject to the tax. In 1798 the tax was levied upon all incomes of £60 and upwards. Since 1875-6 the tax has been levied only upon incomes of £150 and upwards, subject to certain allowances or abatement of duty. Non-income taxpayers, on the other hand, comprise the lower middle class and the labouring classes. The more common distinction of society is the division into the higher, middle, and lower classes. But who are the higher classes? Shall we place within this category the large landowners only, or shall we include among them those having large incomes from whatever sources? Who are the middle classes? There is a higher middle and a lower middle class. Our merchants and bankers pride themselves on being the great middle class. But so are clerks, teachers, and ministers of religion, having but a small annual income; whilst it is a misnomer to distinguish any number of persons as working classes when we are all workers, some with the hand, some with the mind, and many with both. Moreover, the so-called working classes include artisans, labourers, domestic servants, &c., &c. Practically we have four classes of society: first, we may take the aristocracy of wealth including all having an income of £3000 and upwards; second, the middle class, those having an income of £500 to less than £3000; third, the lower middle class, those having an income of £150 and less than £500; and fourth, we have the lower professional or trading classes, and the labouring classes, having an income of less than £150.

5. *Assessed Incomes of the Middle and Higher Classes*, 1851 and 1881.

Let us now see what light the Income Tax Returns give of the distribution of income among those so assessed in 1851 and 1880 respectively. An exact comparison, indeed, cannot be made; for, whilst the classification under Schedule D in 1851 included the incomes of public companies except mines, quarries, ironworks, gasworks, railways, waterworks, canals, &c., which were not assessed under Schedule D until 1866-67, the classification for 1879-80 includes trade and professions only. Still, the comparison in so far as regards the relative incomes at the two periods may be useful. The return relating to Schedule D refers to Great Britain, and for the years 1850-51 and 1879-80, is as follows:—

ESTIMATES OF THE EARNINGS

Incomes.	1850-51.				1879-80.			
	Number assessed.	Amount assessed.	Per cent. of number.	Per cent. of amount.	Number assessed.	Amount assessed.	Per cent. of number.	Per cent. of amount.
		£				£		
Middle Classes.								
£150 to £200	39,475	6,247,000	35·73	12·01	144,158	22,636,000	40·84	15·10
200 to 300	29,389	6,487,000	26·60	12·47	97,410	21,607,000	27·60	14·43
300 to 400	14,399	4,605,000	13·03	8·85	43,556	13,822,000	12·32	9·22
400 to 500	6,968	2,943,000	6·31	5·65	18,059	7,493,000	5·11	5·00
	90,231	20,282,000	81·67	38·98	303,183	65,658,000	85·89	43·75
Higher Middle Classes.								
500 to 600	5,119	2,638,000	4·63	5·07	12,364	6,324,000	3·50	4·23
600 to 700	2,851	1,768,000	2·58	3·39	7,498	4,697,000	2·12	3·06
700 to 800	1,932	1,405,000	1·74	2·70	4,474	3,233,000	1·27	2·16
800 to 900	1,594	1,306,000	1·44	2·51	3,898	3,176,000	1·10	2·11
900 to 1,000	789	731,000	·71	1·45	1,605	1,482,000	0·45	0·98
1,000 to 2,000	4,708	6,098,000	4·26	11·72	11,495	14,692,000	3·26	9·81
2,000 to 3,000	1,342	3,108,000	1·22	5·97	3,474	7,962,000	0·98	5·32
	18,335	17,054,000	16·58	32·81	44,808	41,466,000	9·68	27·67
Higher Classes.								
3,000 to 4,000	625	2,070,000	·56	3·97	1,600	5,284,000	0·45	3·54
4,000 to 5,000	338	1,446,000	·36	2·78	861	3,731,000	0·24	2·49
5,000 to 10,000	588	3,993,000	·53	7·67	1,604	10,594,000	0·45	7·07
10,000 to 50,000	312	5,289,000	·28	10·47	910	16,056,000	1·26	10·72
50,000 and upwards	26	1,880,000	·02	3·62	77	7,126,000	0·02	4·76
	1,889	14,678,000	1·75	28·51	5,052	42,791,000	1·43	28·58
Total ...	110,455	52,014,000	100·00	100·00	353,043	149,835,000	100·00	100·00

Some interesting facts may be gathered from this table. First, that the average amount of assessments of incomes £150 and upwards in Schedule D per person was £424 in 1880, against £470 in 1851, indicating greater diffuseness of incomes side by side with a larger total. Secondly, that a larger proportion, viz., 85·6 per cent. in 1881, against 80·9 per cent. in 1850-51—are now assessed with the lower incomes than with the larger; and, thirdly, that a larger proportion of the amount—viz., 43 per cent. in 1880, against 38 per cent. in 1881—is assessed on the lower incomes than on the higher.

Comparing the proportion of persons assessed with the population of Great Britain at the respective periods—viz. 20,900,000 in 1851, and 29,800,000 in 1881—the following are the results :—

Income	Number assessed per 1,000,000 inhabitants				Increase per cent.
	1850-1		1879-80		
	Schedule D	All Income Taxpayers	Schedule D	All Income Taxpayers	
Middle Classes.					
£100 to £200	1,900	5,700	4,800	14,400	152
200 to 300	1,980	4,140	3,233	9,699	136
300 to 400	660	1,980	1,466	4,398	122
400 to 500	333	999	600	1,800	80
	4,273	12,819	10,099	30,297	136
Higher Middle Classes.					
500 to 600	101	303	412	1,236	308
600 to 700	135	405	250	750	85
700 to 800	92	276	150	450	63
800 to 900	76	228	130	390	71
900 to 1,000	37	111	53	159	43
1,000 to 2,000	224	672	383	1,149	71
2,000 to 3,000	64	192	115	345	79
	729	2,187	1,493	4,479	104
Higher Classes.					
3,000 to 4,000	29	87	53	159	82
4,000 to 5,000	16	48	28	84	75
5,000 to 10,000	28	84	53	159	96
10,000 to 50,000	15	45	30	90	100
50,000 and upwards	1	3	2	6	100
	89	267	166	498	86
Total . .	5,091	15,273	11,758	35,274	133

Absolutely, as well as in proportion to population, there has been a greater increase in the number of persons in the receipt of the lower than of the higher incomes. These facts apply only to incomes from industry, yet there is reason to believe that they represent the condition of all descriptions of incomes. In a note in the appendix to Mr. Dudley Baxter's paper on national incomes, by Mr. Gripper, of the Inland Revenue, it is stated that the number of income taxpayers under Schedule A may be taken to be divided in the same proportion as under Schedule D; and that the same may be said as to Schedules B, C, and E. Assuming this to be true, it is a significant fact that whilst the number of persons in the receipt of incomes from £150 to £500 increased in the thirty years at the rate of 136 per cent., the number of persons in the receipt of incomes of £3000 and upwards increased only at the rate of 86 per cent.

6. *Relation of Land to other Sources of Wealth.*

It has been asserted in Mr. Henry George's work on "Progress and Poverty," that the effect of an increasing population upon the distribution of wealth is to increase rent, and consequently to diminish the proportion of the produce which goes to capital and labour; and that the reason why, in spite of the increase of productive power, wages constantly tend to a minimum which gives but a bare living, is that with the increase of productive power rent tends to even greater increase, thus producing a constant tendency to force down wages. What has been the proportion of rent of land to the total income of the nation? Have landowners and farmers flourished, and the rest of the people decayed? Let the following comparison of facts answer the question:—

Years	Incomes from land and tithe. Schedule A	Incomes of farmers. Schedule B	Total	Total gross income assessed	Per cent. of Schedules A and B to total income
	£	£	£	£	
1814–5	39,405,000	38,396,000	77,801,000	137,621,000	56
1851	47,800,000	48,000,000	95,800,000	257,000,000	37
1880	69,300,000	69,200,000	138,500,000	577,000,000	24
1882–3	65,957,000	65,823,000	131,780,000	612,836,000	21

The proportion of national income derived from land was therefore considerably less in 1880 than in 1814-5. Who are the real aggressors on the wealth of the country? The landowners have evidently much difficulty in keeping their own, from the decreasing value of land and the inroad of wealthy merchants as purchasers of some of the choicest estates in the market, whilst land companies greatly promote the diffusion of landed property. I shudder to think what a large proportion of the landed property is now mortgaged to the utmost limit of its value. House property has greatly augmented in value. In 1851 the value assessed on houses in Great Britain was £42,978,000; in 1882-3 the value so assessed was £124,728,000. But house property is greatly divided, and building societies have extended the ownership of houses among the labouring classes.

7. *Incomes of the Lower Middle Classes.*

Whatever may have been the increase in the number of persons having comparatively larger incomes, there is reason to believe that a proportionate improvement has also taken place in those immediately below the limit of the income-tax range. Of the lower middle class of life, the Teacher and the Clergyman are the fittest representatives. Of the income of Teachers we have some well-ascertained evidence in the reports of the Committee of Council on Education. Comparing 1855 with 1881, the incomes of Certificated Masters were as follows:—

Masters	Average amount of salaries of certificated teachers		
	1855	1881	Per cent. increase
	£ s. d.	£ s. d.	
Church of England . .	87 19 3	114 8 10	29
British Schools . . .	101 16 7	132 3 3	29
Roman Catholics . .	75 12 5	99 15 0	32
	88 6 0	115 0 0	30
School Board Schools .	—	125 13 0	43

The economic condition of teachers has, therefore, immensely improved within the last twenty-five years. Of the income of clergymen I have few reliable facts, but we know that considerable efforts have been made, and with tolerable success, to increase the stipends of curates, whilst in every religious community the learning and piety of their religious teachers are better appreciated and remunerated. An evidence of this may be given in the rise which has taken place in the stipends of ministers in a comparatively small Church—the

Presbyterian Church of England. In 1866 the average stipend of its ministers was £213. In 1883 their stipends had risen to an average of £310, showing an increase of 45 per cent. The income of commercial and banking clerks may be taken to have increased about 15 per cent., and from facts contributed by two important houses, I learn that the higher salaries of heads of departments have increased considerably more. I have no data to estimate what rise has of late taken place in the income of small shopkeepers, but, judging from the houses they live in, and the rate of their household expenditure, their position must have improved in full proportion to the economic improvement of the people. Nor must I forget the increasing facilities now open to girls and women of the lower middle classes in the Civil Service and other professions to earn at least sufficient for their own maintenance, and so diminish the burden of their parents. Taken altogether, if the average income of the lower middle classes was £90 in 1851, we may fairly take it in 1881 at £110 per family.

8. *Incomes of the Labouring Classes.*

The income of the labouring classes is determined by the wages prevailing in agriculture, building, the manufacturing districts, mining, and in domestic service. Extensive data upon each of these different branches of labour would be necessary in order to estimate carefully the average rise over the whole field. But a few well recorded facts may be given. In Mr. Coleman's Report on Agriculture in Northumberland, appended on the report of the Royal Commission on Agriculture, the single hind's wages per week is given as follows:—

	Wages per week s. d.		Wages per week s. d.
1851	11 0	1871	16 6
1861	16 6	1881	18 0

—showing an increase from 1851 to 1881 of 63 per cent. In Shropshire the price of labour in agriculture was reported as follows:—

	Price of mowing an acre of grass	Price of hoeing an acre of turnips	Price of reaping an acre of corn
1862	3s. to 4s.	5s. to 5s. 6d.	9s. to 10s.
1880	4s. to 7s. 6d.	5s. 6d. to 11s.	13s. to 15s.

In the wages of builders there have been great oscillations. Nominally, the wages of masons, carpenters, &c., have been for some time in London 9d. per hour; but this rate is by no means uniform, and in the country 6½d. to 7d. per hour is commonly the rate. Although the rise which took place in 1882 in building wages has not been uniformly sustained, the position of the building classes has greatly improved, especially where they work by the piece. The wages in the cotton manufacture, as given by Mr. Chadwick in the Journal of the Statistical Society, and by Dr. Watt in the last edition of the " Encyclopædia Britannica," have progressed as follows :—

	1850	1860	1865	1876
	Per week	Per week	Per week	Per week
	s.	s.	s.	s. s.
Spinners (men) . .	20	27	30	35 to 40
Carders . . .	20	28	35	32 to 40
Grinders . . .	14	17	25	25 to 28

In a return produced by Mr. George Lord, President of the Manchester Chamber of Commerce, of the increase of the wages earned in the various trades in Lancashire between the years 1850 and 1883, the total average advance in cotton spinning and weaving, cotton spinning, fine cotton spinning and weaving, bleaching and calico printing, is given at 42 per cent.

And we all know how much the wages of domestic servants have increased. A woman-servant who was content with £10 per annum in 1851, now gets at least £14; and all other descriptions of servants in the same proportion. Not only, however, are the direct wages of working men and women greatly increased of late, but with the extension of piece-work in most industries, their earnings have in many cases become much greater. And, what is more, the income of women and children has greatly increased. Altogether the rise of wages and earnings in all branches of labour has been considerable within the last thirty years, and the income of the workman's family, including every earner in the same, and including the interest on accumulated incomes in the savings bank and other forms, is considerably greater now than in former years. If, therefore, the income of a working man's family in 1851 could fairly be estimated, on the whole number at 20s. a-week, or £52 a-year, the total income of a working man's family in 1881, including the value of perquisites, food, house rent, and clothing, whenever given, may fairly be taken at 32s. per week, or £83 per annum.

9. *Population and Income in* 1851 *and* 1881.

With these facts before us, let us endeavour to take a general view of the income of the people in 1851 and 1881, bearing in mind that the population of the United Kingdom was 27,700,000 in 1851, and 35,200,000 in 1881. The return of the number of persons charged to income tax refers only to those deriving income from trade and professions. How shall we arrive at the number paying Income-tax under the other schedules? As I have already stated, Mr. Gripper, of the Inland Revenue, in a note on the number and average income of income taxpayers in England and Wales, appended to Mr. Dudley Baxter's paper on national income, arrived at the conclusion that the number of persons charged under Schedule D being then 297,000, the total number of income taxpayers could be taken at 900,000, or three times as many. Adopting this method, we come to the conclusion, that the 110,000 persons charged with Income-tax under Schedule D in 1850-51 with incomes of £150 and upwards, would represent 330,000 as the entire number of income taxpayers; and that the 353,000 similarly charged in 1879-80 under Schedule D would represent 1,059,000 as the whole number of income taxpayers. Now multiply these numbers by four-and-half to a family, and we have 1,500,000 in 1850-51, and 4,700,000 in 1879-80, as embraced within the income-taxpaying population. On the other side of the scale, we have the great body of the labouring classes, embracing 70 per cent. of the entire population, or 19,300,000 persons, representing 4,300,000 families, in 1851, and 24,600,000 persons, or 5,400,000 families, in 1881. Take the difference between these two sets of figures, and we have the lower middle classes—viz., 6,900,000 persons, or 1,500,000 families, in 1851, and 5,900,000 persons, or 1,300,000 families, in 1881.

Now place against these numbers the income of each class at the respective period, adding six per cent. for the probably assessable income for Ireland in 1851, not then within the Income Tax, and we have the following results:—

1851.

	Number of persons.	Number of families.	Total gross income.	Income per family.	Proportion p. Cent.
			£	£	
Income taxpayers ...	1,500,000	330,000	272,000,000	824	44
Lower middle class	6,900,000	1,500,000	120,000,000	80	20
Labouring classes ...	19,300,000	4,300,000	224,000,000	52	36
	27,700,000	6,130,000	616,000,000	100	100

OF THE WORKING CLASSES. 55

1879-80.

	Number of persons.	Number of families.	Total gross income.	Income per family.	Proportion p. cent.
Income taxpayers ...	4,700,000	1,060,000	£ 577,000,000*	£ 544	49
Lower middle class	5,900,000	1,300,000	143,000,000	110	12
Labouring classes ...	24,600,000	5,400,000	448,000,000	83	39
	35,200,000	7,760,000	1,168,000,000	150	100

If we now compare the income of these classes of society in 1851 and 1881 we have their rate of progress as follows:—

	1851.	1881.	Increase per cent.	Decrease per cent.
Income taxpayers ...	£ 824	£ 544	—	30
Lower middle classes	80	110	37	—
Labouring classes ...	52	83	59	—
	100	150	42	—

It may seem bold to reduce to a numerical ratio the relative condition of the different classes of society; nevertheless, we have here a clear evidence that the labouring classes have participated to the full in the tide of prosperity which the nation has enjoyed for the last thirty years, and a tangible proof that the increase of commerce and manufactures has not only introduced into the community a powerful middle class, but has actually increased considerably the income of the labouring population. In truth, with prosperous trade, we have progress all along the line.

10. *Progress and Poverty.*

Mr. Henry George's work on progress and poverty is able and ingenious; but the arguments produced do not stand the test of ecomonic science. Still less reliable or economic, however, is the programme of the Democratic Federation recently issued, including, as it does, among other things, the State appropriation of railways, the practical repudiation of the National Debt, and the nationalisation of land. Believe me,

* In 1882-83 the sum assessed was £601,450,000.

there is no short cut in the road to wealth. Let us not deceive ourselves with illusory statements or fanciful doctrines. Make Socialism ever so plain, and it will be found to rest on the negation of the right of property, which is the best incentive to the employment of labour, and on the possibility of an equal division of wealth, which is incompatible with the endless variety of powers and talents of men, and the ever-shifting circumstances of life. All facts recording the economic progress of every class of the people in the United Kingdom bear ample testimony to the truth of economic axioms; and our labouring classes are too intelligent to imagine they can set them at naught, or that they would benefit by the attempt to do so. They know, moreover, that by the working out of economic problems, the financial administration of late years has been altogether in their favour, for, while the taxes on general comforts, such as corn, tea, sugar, coffee, &c., have been either altogether relaxed, or greatly reduced, the taxes on extravagance, as on spirits, tobacco, and wine, have become much more productive. It is, moreover, a source of great comfort to find that, whilst in 1851 the amount held by the savings banks was £30,000,000, in 1882 it reached £84,000,000. Allowing that the amount held by the savings banks belongs to the lower middle and labouring classes alike, it follows that, whilst in 1851 the amount so held averaged £1 2s. 10d. per head, in 1882 it averaged £2 15s., showing an improvement of 139 per cent.*

THE BRITISH REVENUE IN 1842 AND 1882.

	1842.	1882.	Increase.	Decrease.
	£	£	%	%
Taxes on Luxuries: Beer, Spirits, Tobacco, Wine ...	18,100,000	37,300,000	106	—
Taxes on General Comforts: Tea, Sugar, Coffee, Corn, and others	15,800,000	4,800,000	—	69
Taxes on Land, Houses, and Employments	5,800,000	6,600,000	13	—
Taxes on Industries: Paper, Hops	3,200,000	800,000	—	—
Taxes on Transfer of Property Stamps ...	7,300,000	11,300,000	68	—
Revenue from Income and Property Tax ...	—	9,900,000	—	—
,, Post Office and Telegraph ...	1,400,000	8,600,000	514	—
,, Other branches ...	600,000	5,700,000	—	—
Total Revenue ...	52,200,000	85,000,000	—	—

* *The British Revenue* in 1842 and 1882.

11. *Relative Improvement of different Classes of Society.*

The relative condition of classes in the United Kingdom is by no means immutable. Wealth is attainable by labour and economy, and no class is shut out from the competition. Nay, more, under the British political system there is no right, no advantage, and no avenue to honour, which is not free and open to all alike. Let there be only perseverance and economy, talent and wisdom, self-mastery and self-restraint, honour and virtue, and the ascent from the lowest to the highest rank, though often rugged and steep, is barred to no one. What is it that the labouring classes should really aim at? Release from labour? A greater amount of political power? Ah, no! The true elevation of the labouring man consists in an increasing energy of his thinking powers, a greater force of moral purpose, a greater culture of the intellect, a greater refinement of manner and taste, above all in an increasing capacity to repel what is depressing and to attract what is ennobling in his daily intercourse of life.

ESTIMATES OF THE EARNINGS

INCOME TAX. SCHEDULE D.

Return giving the Number of Persons and Gross Amount of Profits assessed under Schedule D in Great Britain, distinguished in the following Classes for the Years 1850-1 and 1879-80.*

	GREAT BRITAIN.				
	1850-51.†		1879-80.‡		
	Number.	Gross Amount Assessed.	Number.	Gross Amount Assessed.	
		£		£	
£100 to £150, but not exempt.	33,867	2,510,828	45,792	4,309,788	Under £150, but not exempt.
150 to 200	39,475	6,247,277	144,158	22,636,446	150 to 200
200 ,, 300	29,389	6,487,327	97,410	21,607,602	200 ,, 300
300 ,, 400	14,399	4,605,167	43,556	13,821,549	300 ,, 400
400 ,, 500	6,968	2,942,631	18,059	7,492,711	400 ,, 500
500 ,, 600	5,119	2,638,215	12,364	6,323,612	500 ,, 600
600 ,, 700	2,851	1,767,978	7,498	4,597,229	600 ,, 700
700 ,, 800	1,932	1,405,372	4,474	3,232,729	700 ,, 800
800 ,, 900	1,594	1,305,509	3,898	3,175,785	800 ,, 900
900 ,, 1,000	789	730,670	1,605	1,482,255	900 ,, 1,000
1,000 ,, 2,000	4,708	6,097,786	11,495	14,692,200	1,000 ,, 2,000
2,000 ,, 3,000	1,342	3,108,302	3,474	7,962,096	2,000 ,, 3,000
3,000 ,, 4,000	625	2,070,526	1,600	5,284,754	3,000 ,, 4,000
4,000 ,, 5,000	338	1,446,531	861	3,731,024	4,000 ,, 5,000
5,000 ,, 10,000	588	3,993,335	1,604	10,594,777	5,000 ,, 10,000
10,000 ,, 50,000	312	5,289,076	910	16,056,337	10,000 ,, 50,000
50,000 and upwards.	26	1,879,794	77	7,125,916	50,000 and upwards.
	144,322	54,526,324	398,835	154,126,810	

* The following return has been most kindly contributed by the Commissioners of the Inland Revenue. It differs from the corresponding returns of the 13th and 24th Reports of that Board in the fact that the amount given in this return is the amount *assessed*, whilst the amount given in these returns is the amount *charged* to income tax. The difference between the two is considerable as regards all incomes subject to abatements and allowances.

† This classification includes the incomes of public companies, except mines, quarries, ironworks, gasworks, railways, waterworks, canals, &c., which were not assessed under Schedule D until 1866-7.

‡ This classification includes trades and professions only, there being no similar classification of public companies on record. The amount for such public companies as it is assumed were included in the classification for 1850-51, was, for the year 1879-80, £30,470,000.

Gross Amount of Property and Profits under all Schedules in Great Britain in the Years 1850-51 and 1879-80.

1850-51	...	... £257,392,723	... ...	Great Britain
1879-80	...	... £540,756,324	... ...	,,
		36,140,577	... ...	Ireland
Total	...	... £576,896,901	... ...	United Kingdom

CHAPTER IV.
APPROPRIATION OF WAGES AND OTHER INCOMES.

SECTION 1.
WHAT HAS BECOME OF THE INCREASE OF EARNINGS FROM 1867 TO 1883.

THE wages and earnings of the working classes were found, in 1867, to reach the gross total of £412,000,000, inclusive of allowances, &c., or £370,000,000 of money income. From 1871 to 1873 a considerable advance in wages took place, amounting to full 20 to 30 per cent., and though since that time there has been a fall in the wages from the highest point, the resources of the working classes are found to have amounted in 1884 to £521,000,000 gross, or £470,000,000 money income, giving an average of £42 14s. 1d. per family in 1884, against an income of £38 per family in 1867. Assuming the income of the working classes in 1867 to have sufficed for their general expenditure, the excess of income should be visible in savings and investments of different kinds. It appears, however, that though some portion of that excess has been saved* the bulk has gone in a much greater consumption of articles of food, drink, clothing, furniture, and in larger payments for rent, education, amusements, &c. In 1867 the value of articles of food and drink imported and consumed was £86,607,000; in 1884 it was £154,874,000. If we take the working classes to number 70 per cent. of the population, and to consume 70 per cent. of the quantities of food and drink imported, it would follow that, whereas in 1867 their expenditure in these items amounted to £61,000,000, or £12·97 per family, in 1881 it amounted to £109,000,000, or £19·44 per family, showing an increase of 49·88 per cent. The prices of these articles were not so much increased, but the quantity consumed was greater.

SECTION 2.
CONSUMPTION OF ALCOHOLIC & NON-ALCOHOLIC BEVERAGES.

IN taking the quantities and values of the articles of food and drink imported and consumed we must bear in mind,

---

* See p. 38, and Appendix, p. 151.

however, that the consumption of such articles as foreign corn, meat, &c., is greatly influenced by the home harvest, and that the prices indicated are those given in the Statistical Abstract, exclusive of any import duties and profits of distribution. It is not, indeed, from the wholesale value, but from the retail prices of the merchandise consumed that we may best arrive at the appropriation of wages and other incomes. And an illustration of this may be given of the expenditure voluntarily incurred in 1867 and 1883, respectively, in alcoholic and non-alcoholic beverages. In 1867 the consumption of alcoholic beverages consisted of 30,875,000 * gallons of British and foreign spirits, equal, at 20s. per gallon, to £30,875,000; of 890,000,000 gallons beer, which, at 1s. 6d. per gallon, gives £67,000,000; and of 13,583,000 gallons wine, which, taking the declared value plus the duty, and adding 20 per cent. for distribution, gives £6,860,000, making a total of £104,735,000. In 1883 the consumption was 36,639,000 gallons British and foreign spirits, equal to £36,639,000; 966,000,000 gallons beer, worth £72,000,000; and 14,195,000 gallons wine, worth £7,366,000, making a total of £116,005,000, showing an increase of 10·47 per cent. In 1867 the consumption of non-alcoholic beverages consisted of 97,000,000 lbs. tea, valued at £12,314,000; 40,000,000 lbs. coffee, valued at £2,011,000; and 7,500,000 lbs. cocoa, valued at £261,000, making a total of £14,586,000. In 1883 the consumption was 279,529,000 lbs. tea, valued at £16,106,000; 45,376,000 lbs. coffee, valued at £2,009,000; and 14,478,000 lbs. cocoa, valued at £573,000, giving a total of £18,688,000, showing an increase of 28·12 per cent. But if we take the consumption and cost of these articles at the two periods per head of the population, we find, as regards alcoholic beverages, that in quantities there was an increase of 8·17 in the consumption of spirits, but a decrease of 8·63 per cent. in the consumption of beer, and of 11·11 per cent. in the consumption of wine; whereas in the case of non-alcoholic beverages, there was an increase of 30·43 per cent. in the consumption of tea, and of 157·14 in the consumption of cocoa; but a decrease of 14·42 per cent. in the consumption of coffee. The amount of expenditure per head, shows a decrease of 1·72 per cent. in alcoholic beverages, but an increase of 5·58 per cent. in the amount devoted to non-alcoholic beverages.

---

* Mr. Hoyle, in his Drink Bill, takes the cost of British Spirits at 20s., of Foreign Spirits at 24s., of wine at 18s., and of beer at 1s. 6d. per gallon.

Section 3.
PROPORTIONAL PERSONAL EXPENDITURE BY THE WORKING, MIDDLE, AND HIGHER CLASSES.

No distinction is made by the Board of Trade and the Inland Revenue Commissioners in their tables as regards the class of consumers. We have in them, however, materials which throw much light on the method of appropriation of wages and other incomes, of which a Committee of the British Association * availed themselves for a report in 1882, which I drew up on their behalf, on the subject, and of which the substance is as follows :—

Though the personal consumption of the labouring classes is scarcely equal to that of the middle and higher classes in quantities and value, the larger number of the labouring classes tends to equalise, in many cases, the total amount of expenditure of both. It is well known, moreover, that whilst beer is more largely consumed by the labouring classes, wine is mainly used by the middle and higher classes; cotton and wool constitute the dress of the labouring classes, linen and silk are more largely used by the middle and higher. Bearing in mind these and other facts, well ascertained, the following may be taken as an approximate division of the expenditure :—

Gross or Personal Expenditure.

	Working Classes.		Middle and Higher Classes.	
	£	Per cent.	£	Per cent.
Food and Drink	299,400,000	71·01	201,000,000	43·84
Dress..	61,800,000	14·66	86,000,000	18·76
House	39,300,000	9·34	77,100,000	16·87
Tobacco	9,200,000	2 18	3,900,000	·85
Education, &c.	4,200,000	1·00	30,800,000	6·72
Amusements..	1,900,000	·45	10,600,000	2·32
Taxes	4,700,000	1·12	42,800,000	9·34
Locomotion	1,000,000	·24	6,000,000	1·30
Cost of distribution..	—	—	—	—
	421,500,000	100	458,200,000	100

If we distribute the expenditure in silk, gold and silver plate, tobacco, beer, spirits, wine, and other luxuries, amounting in all to about £150,000,000 gross amount, between the

---

* Extract of Report of the Committee of the British Association for the Advancement of Science on the Appropriation of Wages and other Incomes. See Transactions of the British Association for 1880, 1881, and 1882.

labouring and middle and higher classes, the proportion may be estimated as follows:—

	Working Classes.	
	Personal Expenditure.	Per Cent.
	£	
Necessaries	336,000,000	80
Luxuries	85,500,000	20
	421,500,000	100
	Middle and Higher Classes.	
Necessaries	394,000,000	86
Luxuries	64,200,000	14
	458,200,000	100

The working classes appear thus to devote a larger proportion of their incomes to luxuries than the middle and higher classes, a fact all the more to be regretted since the working classes are thereby left with so much less available for the necessaries of life. Luxuries may be indulged in after the necessaries of life are fully provided for, and a proportional surplus for saving has been secured. They should not be indulged in at the expense of the necessaries of life, or before a proportional surplus for saving has been secured.

Thus classified we have an average gross or personal expenditure of 28s. per week for each working man's family, and of 73s. a week for each of the middle and higher classes' family, and an average net or national expenditure of 23s. for each workman's family, and 55s. for each middle and higher class family.

In the previous report the income of the people of the United Kingdom was estimated as follows:—

	Assessed for Income-tax.	Charged.
	£	£
Income of the Middle and Higher Classes	578,046,297	490,425,774
Income of Non-Income-tax Payers, Lower Middle and Working Classes	500,000,000	500,000,000

OF THE WORKING CLASSES. 63

Assuming the average income of the working classes at 30s. per week per family, including two earners each, their total earnings would amount to £430,000,000, leaving £70,000,000 as the income of the lower middle class. The classification made of the expenditure renders it necessary to take the income of the working classes separately, and, by placing the income against the expenditure, we have the following results:—

	Working Classes.	Middle and Higher Classes.
	£	£
Income	430,000,000	578,000,000
Expenditure	421,000,000	458,000,000
Excess	9,000,000	120,000,000

We have hitherto dealt with the personal expenditure as a matter of a more or less voluntary character. But immediately attached to it is the important item of taxation, and to it we must devote special attention.

SECTION 4.

INCIDENCE OF TAXATION.*

THE incidence of taxation is a subject of great interest and difficulty, and has of late attracted considerable attention. Are the working classes unduly weighted with the burden of taxes? Within the last 30 years a great reduction has been made in taxes on general comforts, whilst an increasing revenue has been received from articles of luxury. Taxation does no longer cripple the consumption of articles of food; no longer restricts the import of raw materials; no longer interferes with the industries of the people. The principal amount comes from luxuries, and from sources which are no burden to anyone. And this altered method of raising a revenue has had considerable influence on the incidence of taxation on the different classes of the community. Assuming the working classes to include 70 per cent. of the population, and the middle and higher classes 30 per cent., the incidence of taxation among them in 1842, 1862, and 1882 respectively may be estimated as follows:—

* Extract from a paper on "Statistics of the Revenue of the United Kingdom from 1859 to 1882" read at the Statistical Society, December 18th, 1883. See "Journal of Statistical Society," 1884.

ESTIMATES OF THE EARNINGS

[000's omitted.]

Taxes.	1842.			1862.			1882.		
	Total.	Middle and Higher Classes.	Working Classes.	Total.	Middle and Higher Classes.	Working Classes.	Total.	Middle and Higher Classes.	Working Classes.
	£	£	£	£	£	£	£	£	£
Sugar	5,300,	1,600,	3,700,	6,400,	1,900,	4,500,	—	—	—
Tea	3,900,	1,200,	2,700,	5,500,	1,600,	3,900,	4,000,	1,000,	3,000,
Coffee	900,	900,	—	400,	400,	—	200,	200,	—
Corn	600,	200,	400,	800,	200,	600,	—	—	—
Other imported articles	5,000,	1,700,	3,300,	1,200,	400,	800,	700,	200,	500,
Other exciseable articles	3,500,	1,000,	2,500,	1,300,	400,	900,	800,	200,	600,
Spirits	7,600,	2,300,	5,300,	12,300,	3,700,	8,600,	18,400,	5,400,	13,000,
Malt	5,300,	1,600,	3,700,	5,900,	1,800,	4,100,	8,600,	2,600,	6,000,
Wine	1,700,	1,700,	—	1,100,	1,100,	—	1,400,	1,400,	—
Tobacco	3,500,	1,000,	2,500,	5,600,	1,700,	3,900,	8,800,	2,600,	6,200,
Licences	1,400,	400,	1,000,	1,600,	500,	1,100,	3,600,	1,600,	2,000,
Assessed taxes	1,300,	900,	400,	1,100,	800,	300,	—	—	—
Land and house tax	3,000,	2,500,	500,	1,900,	1,400,	500,	3,500,	3,000,	500,
Stamps	7,300,	7,300,	—	8,600,	8,600,	—	11,400,	11,400,	—
Property and Income tax	—	—	—	10,400,	10,400,	—	9,900,	9,900,	—
	50,200,	24,200,	26,000,	64,100,	34,900,	29,200,	71,300,	39,500,	31,800,

If we compare the number of persons of the different classes with the relative amount of public taxes without local taxes, the following are the results:—

Public Taxes.

	1842. Per Head.	1862. Per Head.	1882. Per Head.
	£ s. d.	£ s. d.	£ s. d.
Middle and Higher Classes	3 0 0	3 17 8	3 6 0
Working Classes	1 7 4	1 9 0	1 5 11

But add the local taxation for the year 1882, and estimate the same to fall in the proportion of two-thirds on the middle and higher classes and one-third on the working classes, the result will be as follows:—

	Total.	Middle and Higher Classes.	Working Classes.
	£	£	£
Public Taxes	71,000,000	39,500,000	31,500,000
Local ,, ...	39,000,000	26,000,000	13,000,000
	110,000,000	65,500,000	44,500,000
Per Head	£3 2s. 10d.	£6 4s. 8d.	£1 15s. 11d.

And if we compare the taxation bearing upon these different classes of society with their respective incomes the results are as follows:—

	Income.	Taxation.	Percentage.
	£	£	
Income Tax Assessment and Income of the Lower Middle Class not assessed	720,000,000	65,500,000	9·09
Money Income of Labouring Classes	470,000,000	44,500,000	9·46
	1,190,000,000	110,000,000	9·24

Relatively to income, a slightly greater amount of burden appears to weigh upon the labouring classes than upon the higher and middle classes. But while the taxation of the higher and middle class can with scarcity be evaded, that of the labouring classes, being mostly on alcoholic liquors or on tobacco, is in many cases wholly avoided; it being quite optional on their part to consume spirits, beer, or tobacco. Thus, as a matter of fact, temperance families, and those who do not smoke, are exempt from a large portion of the public taxes.

The duty of paying taxes devolves on all the subjects of a State quite irrespective of their income and position in society, for they are required not only for the protection and safeguard of property, but for the secure enjoyment of rights and privileges, in which the labouring man and the poor are as much interested as the rich. In the glorious charter of national greatness all have an equal share. Where would be the independence; where the natural pride of the great mass of our sturdy workmen, did they not feel that they contribute their share towards maintaining and uplifting the honour and glory of their fatherland? Much may remain to be done with a view to a still more equitable and convenient distribution of taxes, but there is no reason to believe that the working classes are burdened with any undue share of the burden of the nation.

IMPORTS AND CONSUMPTION OF ARTICLES OF FOOD AND DRINK.

	1867.			1883.		
	Quantity consumed per head.	Prices.	Declared Value of Imports less Exports.	Quantity consumed per head.	Prices.	Declared Value of Imports less Exports.
			£			£
Bacon and Hams	1·92 lb.	s. 51·86 per cwt.	1,392,000	10·96 lb.	s. 53·08 cwt.	10,036,000
Beef	...	£ 50·52 "	623,000	...	52·91 "	2,894,000
Butter	4·19 "	£ 5·13 "	5,854,000	7·18 "	£ 5·04 "	11,774,000
Cheese	3·32 "	2·82 "	2,555,000	5·51 "	2·72 "	4,890,000
Cocoa	0·14 "	d. 6·96 per lb.	218,000	0·36 "	d. 7·97 lb.	478,000
Coffee	1·04 "	£ 3·55 per cwt.	1,328,000	0·89 "	£ 3·51 owt.	1,506,000
Corn, Wheat	141·06 "	s. 14·42 "	41,324,000	250·77	s. 9·81 "	67,210,000
Eggs	13·19 "	d. 7·16 per doz.	990,000	26·40	d. 8·37 doz.	2,732,000
Fish	...	s. 22·06 per owt.	497,000	4·01 "	s. 35·53 owt.	2,302,000
Fruit	3·96 "	s. 18·15 to 28·74	2,303,000	4·47 "	s. 27·72 "	2,127,000
Lard	...	s. 50·66 per owt.	625,000	...	s. 52·65 "	2,247,000
Pork	...	s. 46·83 "	352,000	...	s. 40·43 "	762,000
Potatoes	5·10 "	s. 5·78 "	397,000	16·17 "	s. 6·16 "	1,585,000
Rice	5·85 "	s. 14·64 "	1,160,000	12·45 "	s. 8·20 "	1,356,000
Spices { Cinnamon Pepper	...	20·59 3·54	} 27,000	...	{ d. 13·61 lb. 6·42	} 923,000
Spirits, Rum	0·28 Galls.	2·02	1,765,000	0·23 Galls.	s. 1·86 galls.	1,274,000
Sugar	40·58 Raw	21·80	11,509,000	71·74 Raw & ref'd.] 20·10 owt.		24,357,000
Tea	3·68 "	d. 18·87 per lb.	7,603,000	4·80 lb.	d. 12·46 lb.	9,148,000
Tobacco, unmftd	1·35 "	7·68	1,841,000	1·42 "	7·78 "	2,413,000
Wine	0·45 Galls.	6·26	4,244,000	0·40 Galls.	s. 7·01 galls.	4,870,000
			£86,607,000			£154,884,000

OF THE WORKING CLASSES.

CONSUMPTION & COST OF ALCOHOLIC & NON-ALCOHOLIC BEVERAGES MAY BE CALCULATED AS FOLLOWS:—

ALCOHOLIC DRINKS.

	1867.	£		1883.	£
Spirits, British, 21,590,000 gallons, at 20s.	...	21,590,000	Spirits, British, 29,422,000 gallons, at 20s.	...	29,422,000
,, Foreign, 9,283,000 gallons, at 20s.	...	9,283,000	,, Foreign, 7,217,000 gallons, at 20s.	...	7,217,000
Beer, 47,891,000, Malt, &c., 1,528,000, Sugar, equal to 890,000,000 gallons, at 1s. 6d.	...	67,000,000	Beer, 966,000,000 gallons, at 1s. 6d.	...	72,000,000
Wine, 13,583,000 gallons	...	4,244,000	Wine, 14,195,000 gallons	...	4,870,000
Duty on declared value	...	1,476,000	Duty	...	1,268,000
20 per cent. Distribution	5,720,000		20 per cent. Distribution	6,138,000	
	1,140,000	6,860,000		1,228,000	7,365,000
		£104,735,000			£116,003,000

NON-ALCOHOLIC DRINKS.

	1867.	£		1883.	£
Tea, 97,000,000 lbs., value	...	7,603,000	Tea, 279,529,000 lbs, value	...	9,148,000
Duty	...	2,659,000	Duty	...	4,269,000
20 per cent. Distribution		10,262,000	20 per cent. Distribution		13,417,000
		2,052,000			2,683,000
Coffee, 40,146,000 lbs., value	...	1,328,000	Coffee, 45,376,000 lbs., value	...	1,505,000
Duty	...	348,000	Duty	...	194,000
20 per cent. Distribution		1,676,000	20 per cent. Distribution		1,699,000
		335,000			340,000
Cocoa, 7,537,000 lbs., value	...	218,000	Cocoa, 14,478,000 lbs., value	...	478,000
Duty	...	22,000	Duty	...	65,000
20 per cent. Distribution		240,000	20 per cent. Distribution		543,000
		48,000			108,000
		288,000			651,000
		£14,613,000			£18,766,000

THE QUANTITIES CONSUMED AND THE AMOUNT OF EXPENDITURE PER HEAD AT THE RESPECTIVE PERIODS.

QUANTITIES CONSUMED PER HEAD.

Alcoholic Beverages.

	1867.	1883.	Percentage.	
	Gallons.	Gallons.	Increase.	Decrease.
Spirits—British	0·71	0·83		
Foreign	0·28	0·23		
	0·98	1·06	8·17	
Beer	29·66	27·1		8·63
Wine	0·45	0·40		11·11

Non-Alcoholic Beverages.

	1867. lbs.	1883. lbs.	Increase.	Decrease.
Tea	3·68	4·80	30·43	
Coffee	1·04	0·89		14·42
Cocoa	0·14	0·36	157·14	

AMOUNT EXPENDED PER HEAD.

Alcoholic Beverages.

	1867. Per head. £ s. d.	1883. Per head. £ s. d.	Percentage. Increase.	Decrease.
Spirits	1 0 7	1 0 4		
Beer	2 4 8	2 0 0		
Wine	0 4 6	0 4 1		
	3 9 9	3 4 5		7·27

Non-Alcoholic Beverages.

	1867. Per head. £ s. d.	1883. Per head. £ s. d.	Increase.	Decrease.
Tea	0 8 2	0 8 11		
Coffee and Cocoa	0 1 6	0 0 11		
	0 9 8	0 9 10	1·72	

OF THE WORKING CLASSES. 69

Estimate of Gross or Personal Expenditure.
(The Italics indicate articles of luxury.)

	Total.	Working Classes.		Middle and Higher Classes.	
		Amount.	Per cent. of Total.	Amount.	Per cent. of Total.
Food and Drink:—	£	£		£	
Bread	77,500,000	50,800,000	66	26,700,000	34
Potatoes	33,200,000	22,000,000	66	11,200,000	34
Vegetables	17,000,000	11,200,000	66	5,800,000	34
Meat	99,800,000	50,000,000	50	49,800,000	50
Fish	14,500,000	8,700,000	60	5,800,000	40
Butter and Cheese	36,000,000	21,600,000	60	14,400,000	46
Milk and Eggs	42,000,000	16,800,000	40	25,200,000	60
Fruit	11,100,000	3,300,000	30	7,800,000	70
Sugar	27,000,000	17,800,000	66	9,200,000	34
Tea	15,300,000	10,100,000	66	5,200,000	34
Coffee	3,000,000	—	—	3,000,000	100
Beer	75,000,000	56,200,000	75	18,800,000	25
Spirits	40,000,000	30,000,000	75	10,000,000	25
Wine	9,000,000	900,000	10	8,100,000	90
	500,400,000	299,400,000	60	201,000,000	40
Dress:—					
Cotton	31,000,000	15,500,000	50	15,500,000	50
Wool	63,000,000	31,500,000	50	31,500,000	50
Linen	7,700,000	800,000	10	6,900,000	90
Silk	17,600,000	1,800,000	10	15,800,000	90
Leather	23,500,000	11,700,000	50	11,800,000	50
Silver Plate & Jewellery	5,000,000	500,000	10	4,500,000	90
	147,800,000	61,800,000	42	86,000,000	58
House:—					
House Rent	71,700,000	28,700,000	40	43,300,000	60
Furniture	11,000,000	2,200,000	20	8,800,000	80
Coal	15,000,000	6,000,000	40	9,000,000	60
Gas	13,700,000	1,400,000	10	12,300,000	90
Water	5,000,000	1,000,000	20	4,000,000	80
	116,400,000	39,300,000	35	77,100,000	65
Tobacco	13,100,000	9,200,000	70	3,900,000	30
Education	11,000,000	1,100,000	10	9,900,000	90
Literature	7,000,000	1,400,000	20	5,600,000	80
Newspapers	5,000,000	500,000	10	4,500,000	90
Church	12,000,000	1,200,000	10	10,800,000	90
	35,000,000	4,200,000	12	30,800,000	88
Locomotion	7,000,000	1,000,000	14	6,000,000	86
Theatres	6,500,000	1,000,000	15	5,500,000	85
Amusements	6,000,000	900,000	15	5,100,000	85
	12,500,000	1,900,000	15	10,600,000	85
Taxes	47,500,000	4,700,000	10	42,800,000	90
Total	879,700,000	421,500,000	48	458,200,000	52

WAGES AND EARNINGS OF THE WORKING CLASSES.

ESTIMATES OF THE EARNINGS OF THE WORKING CLASSES. 73

CLASS I.—PROFESSIONAL.

ORDER I.

PERSONS ENGAGED IN THE GENERAL OR LOCAL GOVERNMENT OF THE COUNTRY.

(a) *National Government.*

ARTIFICERS AND LABOURERS IN HER MAJESTY'S DOCKYARDS.

SUB-ORDER 1.

IN the Royal Dockyards the number of workmen authorised for the establishment, in the Estimates for 1883-4, was 18,500.

The advantages enjoyed by the artificers in the Royal Dockyards are given as follows:—They have regular and uninterrupted work throughout the year; work chiefly under cover; forty hours' work per week, or eight hours per day; holidays for which no deduction of pay is made; medical attendance; half-pay when hurt at duty; superannuation after ten years' service; pensions to widows of men killed in the service, and promotion to the highest class of officers in their respective trades. Hired men enjoy all the above advantages, with the following exceptions, viz., some of them are liable to be discharged on completion of certain work, superannuation, pensions to widows, and promotion.

	Establishment Wages per day.	Hired Workmen per day.
Block Makers, 1st Class	5/3	4/ to 4/10
,, ,, 2nd ,,	4/9	...
Block Mills, Leading Men	7/3	3/ to 3/6
Workmen, 1st Class	4/3	...
,, 2nd ,,	3/9	...
,, 3rd ,,	3/3	...
Boiler Makers, Leading Men	8/9	8/ to 10/
,, Ordinary	5/ to 6/8	4/6 ,, 7/6
Braziers and Tinmen	4/9	4/ ,, 5/
Bricklayers	4/6	4/ ,, 4/6
Caulkers, Leading Men	6/ to 7/	4/ ,, 5/4
,, Ordinary	5/	...
Coppersmiths, Leading Men	8/ to 9/6	8/ to 10/
,, Ordinary	5/ ,, 6/6	4/ ,, 6/6
Engine Keepers	4/3	...
Fitters' Draughtsmen	6/ to 7/	...
,, Leading Men	8/ ,, 9/	8/ to 10/

ESTIMATES OF THE EARNINGS

	Establishment Wages per day.	Hired Workmen per day.
Fitters, Ordinary Ship Branch	5/ „ 7/	4/ „ 8/
„ Steam Branch	5/ „ 7/	...
Founders, Leading Men	8/ „ 9/	8/ to 10/
„ Ordinary	4/9 „ 7/	4/ „ 7/6
Hose Makers	3/3 „ 3/9	...
Joiners, Single-Stationed	5/ „ 5/6	...
„ Leading Men	6/ „ 6/6	...
„ Ordinary	4/6	2/10 to 4/10
Labourers, Single Stationed	3/2 to 3/6	...
„ Leading Men, Special	5/6	8/6 to 6/
„	4/ to 4/9	2/6 „ 2/10
„ Skilled	3/3 „ 4/	3/ „ 4/6
„ Ordinary	3/8	...
Locksmiths	4/9	4/ to 4/6
Masons	4/6	3/ „ 3/4
Metal Mills and Sheathing Nail Shops—		
Leading Men	7/3 to 7/9	...
Workmen	3/3 „ 6/3	...
Oar Machine, Oar Finishers	4/ „ 5/	...
Saw Sharpeners	4/	...
Machine Labourers	5/6	...
Oar Makers	5/6	...
Packing Case Maker	5/6	...
Painter, Glazier, and Grinder—		
Single Stationed Men	5/2	3/ to 5/
Leading Men, 1st Class	5/2 to 7/2	...
Workmen	4/2 „ 4/6	...
Pattern Makers, Leading Men	8/ „ 9/	8/ to 10/
„ Ordinary	5/ „ 6/6	4/ „ 7/
Plumbers, Leading Men	5/9 „ 6/3	...
„ Ordinary	4/9	4/ to 5/
Riggers, Coxswain to Staff Captain	4/ to 4/3	4/
Signalmen and Look-out Men	2/6 „ 3/	...
Leading Men	5/6 „ 6/	...
Ordinary	4/ „ 4/3	...
Ropemakers, Leading Men	5/2 „ 5/8	...
„ Ordinary	4/2 „ 4/6	3/10 to 4/2
„ Key Bearer at Ropeyard	3/3	...
Sail Makers, Leading Men	5/2 to 5/8	...
„ Ordinary	4/2 „ 4/6	3/10 to 4/2
Saw Mill, Ordinary	3/3 „ 4/	3/ to 4/6
Sawyers' Topmen	4/2	4/2
„ Pitmen	3/8	3/8
Shipwrights' Draughtsmen	6/ to 7/	...
„ Modellers	7/	...
„ Liner of Masts	7/ to 7/6	...
„ Single-Stationed Men	5/6 „ 6/	...
„ Leading Men	6/ „ 7/	...
„ Ordinary	5/	4/ to 5/4
Stokers, Ordinary	3/9	...
Storehouse Men, Leading Men	6/ to 7/6	...
„ Ordinary	5/ 5/6 & 3/9 to 4/9	...
Smiths, Ordinary	4/9 to 7/6	3/6 to 7/6
„ Hammermen	3/6 „ 4/	3/ „ 4/
Wheelwrights	4/6 „ 5/	2/6 „ 4/10
Apprentices	6d. „ 2/6	...
Boys	1/ „ 2/6	...

POST-OFFICE.

THE number employed in the Post-office is upwards of 17,000. The wages of letter-carriers are given as follows:—

Town letter-carriers, 1st class	26s. to 30s.
,, ,, 2nd class	20s. to 25s.
Suburban, 1st class	23s.
,, 2nd class	20s.
Edinburgh establishment	18s. to 23s.
Dublin ,,	18s. to 20s.
Supplementary	18s.

Letter-carriers are entitled to a retiring pension after service of ten years. They receive a uniform, which costs £4 15s. 4d., and they have Christmas and other gratuities estimated at £13 per annum. They have, moreover, a fortnight's leave of absence annually without deduction of wages; full wages during absence in consequence of accidents incurred in the service; assistance in the insurance of their lives, and medical attendance and medicine gratuitously supplied, both at the office and at their own houses.

(b) *Local Government.*

POLICE.

SUB-ORDER 2.

ACCORDING to the judicial statistics for the year 1883 the number and cost of the police force were as follows:—

	Number.	Cost.
England and Wales	34,488	£3,367,678
Scotland	3,932	341,662
Ireland	15,228	1,719,961
	53,648	5,429,301

The cost, however, includes salaries and pay; allowances and contingent expenses; clothing and accoutrements; superannuation and gratuities; horses, harness, forage, &c.; buildings, station-house charges; printing, stationery, &c.; and other miscellaneous charges.

The weekly wages of constables and sergeants in the police force in England and Wales are given in the Reports of

Inspectors of Constabulary, Police, Counties and Boroughs, 1884, from which are the following :—

Counties.	Constables.	Sergeants.
Bedford	25/1 to 28/7	29/2 to 32/8
Cambridge	21/7 „ 27/5	27/5 „ 30/11
Chester	23/11 „ 29/2	30/4 „ 33/10
Cornwall	20/5 „ 23/4	28/ „ 29/2
Durham	24/6 „ 28/7	29/2 „ 34/5
Gloucester	20/5 „ 23/4	28/ „ 29/2
Lancaster	25/8 „ 39/11	32/2 „ 35/7
Leicester	22/ „ 29/1	27/9 „ 30/1
Lincoln	24/ „ 29/	30/ „ 32/
Surrey	22/9 „ 29/2	29/9 „ 33/3
York, North Riding ...	24/6 „ 29/2	30/4 „ 34/5
York, West Riding ...	23/11 „ 29/2	30/4 „ 33/10
Boroughs.		
Bristol	22/ „ 35/	30/11 „ 33/3
Derby	24/ „ 30/	30/ „ 34/
Liverpool	26/8 „ 31/4 ... Insp.	30/10 „ 49/4
Manchester	24/ „ 32/6	33/ „ 37/
Newcastle-on-Tyne ...	24/ „ 29/	30/ „ 38/
Nottingham	23/ 32/10	30/7 „ 37/3

Order II.

PERSONS ENGAGED IN THE DEFENCE OF THE COUNTRY.

ARMY.

Sub-Order 1.

The Army Estimates for 1884-5 gave the regimental pay, allowances, &c., at £4,500,000. To this should be added the cost of the clothing establishment, provisions, barrack establishment, Divine service, martial law and hospital establishment services and supplies, amounting in all to £7,304,000. Some portion of this amount, however, does not go to the soldiers themselves; and the amount so appropriated for the Army auxiliary and reserve forces cannot be taken at more than £6,000,000.

A Return moved by Mr. Pell in 1878 (182) gave the estimated equivalent weekly wage of a private soldier in the Royal Horse Artillery, the Life and Horse Guards, the Cavalry of the Line, the Royal Engineers, the Foot Guards, and the Infantry, including provisions, clothing, &c.; showing, also, his maximum possible earnings and necessary outgoings as follows :—

—	Household Cavalry.	Cavalry of the Line.	Royal Horse Artillery.	Royal Artillery, Field.	Royal Artillery, Garrison.	Royal Engineers, Dismounted.	Royal Engineers, Mounted.	Foot Guards.	Infantry of the Line.
	£ s. d.	£ s. d.	£ s. d.	£ s. d.	£ s. d.	£ s. d.	£ s. d.	£ s. d.	£ s. d.
Regimental Pay	31 11 2	21 5 10	24 6 8	22 1 0½	22 1 0½	20 1 7½	24 6 8	19 15 5	18 5 0
Provisions	9 12 6	9 12 6	9 12 6	9 12 6	9 12 6	9 12 6	9 12 6	9 12 6	9 12 6
Allowance for Lodging, including Fuel and Light, Barrack Stores, Bedding, and Maintenance of Barracks...	6 1 8	6 1 8	6 1 8	6 1 8	6 1 8	6 1 8	6 1 8	6 1 8	6 1 8
Good Conduct Pay (being the average charge for the total number of Rank and File)	1 5 3	1 5 3	1 5 3	1 5 3	1 5 3	1 5 3	1 5 3	1 5 3	1 5 3
Working Pay ...	...	...	...	...	...	15 12 0	...		...
Clothing	6 17 8	3 19 8	3 17 3	3 16 4	3 13 4	4 7 7	6 1 2	4 6 8	2 19 5
Medical Attendance (being the charge for the Pay of the Medical Officers divided by the total number of the Army)	1 7 8	1 7 8	1 7 8	1 7 8	1 7 8	1 7 8	1 7 8	1 7 8	1 7 8
Total Charge per Annum ... £	56 15 11	43 12 7	46 11 0	44 4 5½	44 1 5½	58 8 3½	48 14 11	42 9 2	39 11 6
Average Weekly Cost ... £	1 1 10	0 16 9¼	0 17 10¾	0 17 0	0 16 11¼	1 2 5½	0 18 8¾	0 16 3¾	0 13 3¼

Maximum possible Earnings, and necessary Outgoings.

The foregoing statement represents the average maximum amount received by the ordinary private soldier regimentally employed; the extra pay granted for special duties, such as clerking, instruction, &c., is exceptional, and varies with the nature of the work.

In addition to the average rate of Good Conduct Pay, shown in the foregoing statement, the private soldier receives, on his discharge from the Army, or on his passing into the Reserve, out of the Drunkenness Fines Fund, a sum of 10s. for each good conduct stripe earned; and in six years he may then receive 20s.

If the soldier passes to the Reserve on the expiry of his first six years' service, he receives 2d. a day deferred pay, accumulated from 1st April, 1876; should he continue with the colours 12 years, he receives then the accumulated 2d. a day from 1st April, 1876, for a period not exceeding 12 years, plus interest accruing during the second six years on the amount earned during the first six years.

The necessary outgoings are to provide the groceries, vegetables, &c., in addition to the free ration, and to pay for washing (weekly charges), and for hair-cutting, library subscriptions, &c. (monthly charges). In the Cavalry, Artillery, and Engineers these outgoings average 4½d. a day, or 2s. 7½d. a week. In the Foot Guards and Infantry these average 4d. a day, or 2s. 4d. a week. The soldier has also to maintain the free kit given to him on enlistment; the charge upon him depends entirely upon the careful habits, or otherwise, of the individual. The kit itself costs the State as under, and many of the articles are estimated to last several years:—

	£	s.	d.
Infantry	1	9	0
Foot Guards	1	10	0
Cavalry	3	16	0
Artillery, Horse and Field	4	4	0
Artillery Garrison	3	3	0
Engineers	3	11	0

The earning of soldiers and seamen is arrived at by dividing the amount expended by the number of men. But this does not give the net earning of the men. A writer on the State of the British Army in the *Quarterly Review* says:— "Under the existing system a soldier is provided by the State with a uniform, including boots, renewed periodically, but he is often required to pay out of his own pocket for a new pair of trousers, serge frock or forage cap, while it is evident that his two pair of boots annually are not sufficient, and the cost of additional boots and repairs to those which he possesses is defrayed by the man himself. He also, on enlistment, is furnished with a free kit of necessaries, comprising underclothing, knife, fork and spoon, brushes, blacking, braces, razor, towels, soap, &c. The kit he has to keep up at his own expense. It is plain from the above that the soldier is *not* clothed by the State. Neither is he fed by the State, for all he obtains in the shape of ration is 1 lb. of bread and ¾ lb. meat daily. The balance, in the shape of groceries, vegetables, milk, &c., is defrayed out of the messing fund, for which 4d. per day is stopped from his pay. In addition he is charged with washing at ½d. a day, hair-cutting 1d. a month, and barrack damages, for which he is lucky if he gets off with 1d. a month. If he belongs to the library the subscription is 3d. a month.

NAVY.

SUB-ORDER 2.

THE Navy Estimates for 1883-4 gave the cost of petty officers and seamen, coastguard service, and marines as follows :—

30,633 Petty Officers	£2,016,457
4,950 Boys	49,459
4,000 Coastguard Service	184,660
12,400 Marines	382,969
Victuals and clothing	870,400
Total	£3,503,915

The wages of petty officers and leading seamen are as follows :—

	Per annum.	Per annum.
Petty Officers and leading Seamen	£30 8 4	to £127 15 0
Able Ordinary and Second Class Ordinary Seamen	16 14 7	to 28 17 11
Chief Boatmen in charge of Stations	57 15 10	
Boys—First Class	10 12 10	
,, Second Class	9 2 6	
Royal Marine Artillery First Class Sergeants	29 16 10½	
Instructor of Gunnery		
Corporals	50 3 9	
Gunners	21 5 10	to 27 15 1¼

The allowances and privileges of seamen in the Navy in respect to pensions, &c., are the same as those for soldiers in the Army.

Order III.
PERSONS ENGAGED IN PROFESSIONAL OCCUPATIONS.
Sub-Order 1, 8.

This order includes Clergymen, Lawyers, Physicians, Authors, Artists, Actors, Teachers, and Scientific Persons.

Class II.—DOMESTIC.

Order IV.
PERSONS ENGAGED IN DOMESTIC OFFICES OR SERVICES.

DOMESTIC SERVICES.
Sub-Order 1.

The number employed in attendance and domestic service is very considerable. The money wages are given as follows:—

	£		£
General Servants...	8	to	20
Kitchen Maids ...	8	,,	20
Laundry Maids ...	12	,,	24
Dairy Maids ...	13	,,	18
Stillroom Maids ...	10	,,	20
Housemaids ...	10	,,	25
Cooks ...	10	,,	50
Housekeepers ...	30	,,	50
Lady's Maids ...	16	,,	30
Upper Nurses ...	16	,,	25
Steward Boys ..	7	,,	16
Grooms ...	12	,,	35
Footmen ...	16	,,	36
Indoor Menservants	35	,,	50
Under Butlers ...	30	,,	75
Butlers ...	50	,,	80
Valets ...	40	,,	70
Stewards ...	70	,,	150

Generally board and lodging are also given, and in some cases liveries and other advantages.

OTHER SERVICES.
Sub-Order 2.

Under this sub-order are office-keepers, cooks (not domestic), charwomen, and others engaged in service, whose wages, including in most cases board and lodging, are similar to those under the previous sub-order.

OF THE WORKING CLASSES. 81

CLASS III.—COMMERCIAL.

ORDER V.
PERSONS ENGAGED IN COMMERCIAL OCCUPATIONS.

PERSONS ENGAGED IN THE CONVEYANCE OF MEN, ANIMALS, GOODS, AND MESSAGES.

RAILWAYS.

SUB-ORDER 1.

ACCORDING to a return of the number of persons employed by each of the Railway Companies of the United Kingdom on the 31st March, 1884, moved by Mr. Broadhurst (242), the number was as follows:—

Secretaries' Department	1,331
Accountants' ,,	2,841
Legal and Parliamentary Department	222
Traffic Department—	
General Managers'	781
Superintendents'	74,177
Goods Managers'	69,713
	144,671
Locomotive Department	118,326
Engineers' ,,	80,609
Storekeepers' ,,	2,820
Police ,,	1,781
Telegraph ,,	3,754
Steamboat Service, Docks, and Piers	6,041
Canals	1,963
Hotels and Refreshment	2,518
Miscellaneous	889
	367,293

Twelve hours a day is the usual time for work, less two hours allowed for meals, and when night work is required the

F

A Return of the Names of Railways and Rates of Wages paid to Railway Servants was published by the Amalgamated Society of Railway Servants of England, Ireland, Scotland, and Wales, on the principal lines of Great Britain and Ireland, which is summarised as follows:—

	Engineers and Drivers	Firemen	Passenger Guards	Goods Guards	Shunters	Signalmen	Passenger Porters	Goods Porters	Plate Layers
Great Western, Swindon	5/ to 7/6	3/ to 4/6	3/10 to 5/8	3/4 to 5/4	3/8 to 4/2	2/6 to 4/2	2/6 to 3/	2/2 to 3/6	2/2 to 3/
North London, Bow	5/ to 7/6	3/ to 4/6	3/9 to 5/	3/0 to 5/	3/6 to 3/10	3/10 to 5/10	3/	—	3/9
London and N. Westn., Crewe	5/ to 7/6	3/2 to 4/	4/2 to 5/	—	3/4 to 4/8	3/ to 4/8	2/10 to 3/	3/ to 3/6	2/10 to 3,6
North Eastern, Darlington	5/ to 7/	3/ to 4/6	3/8 to 4/6	3/10 to 5/	3/2	3/4 to 4/8	3/2	3/ to 3/6	3/ to 3/4
North British, Edinburgh	4/8 to 6/6	3/2 to 4/	3/6	4/ to 5/	4/ to 5/	3/4 to 3/8	2/11	3/	2/10 to 3/4
Midland, Carlisle	5/6 to 7/6	3/6 to 4/6	3/4 to 4/2	4/ to 5/	3/4 to 3/8	3/2 to 4/	2/4 to 2/8	3/ to 3/6	3/ to 4/
Great Eastern, Norwich	4/6 to 7/6	3/1 to 4/	3/ to 4/8	3/ to 4/8	2/8 to 4/2	2/8 to 3/6	1/8 to 2/8	2/8	2/8 to 3/4
	6/	3/9	4/	4/	3,8	3/4	2,6	2/8	3/1
	£93	£59	£62	£62	£55	£52	£39	£40	£48

men work alternately by relays night and day. In some cases Sunday work goes on. A candidate for the duties of a porter must be 5 feet 7 inches in height; 21, and not exceeding 30 years of age; able to read and write; free from bodily complaint, and must produce testimonials of character.

Goods and passenger guards, signal or pointsmen and porters, are supplied with a suit of uniform annually, and on most lines with an *extra* pair of trousers. Engine drivers and firemen are supplied with an overcoat each every second year on some lines, and every third year on others, and on the L. B. and S. C. they are supplied with a cap as well. There is such a thing as piecework on some railways in the goods traffic under the name of the "trip system," a stipulated sum being given for journeys between certain places. It is not generally approved of by the men, as the amount paid is calculated upon the time a journey can be made under favourable conditions, but when delays occur, and the men are much longer on the road, the sum paid, calculated by the hour, is very small. The wages are given as follows (see Return supplied from the Amalgamated Society of Railway Servants) :—

CARRIERS ON ROADS.

SUB-ORDER 2.

INLAND transport by carts, cabs, omnibuses, &c., is considerable, though the railways are extending on all sides. Comparing the number of men twenty years and upwards respectively engaged in the railways, and as carmen, omnibus-men, &c., with the population in 1851 and 1881 in England and Wales, the number and proportion stood as follows :—

Occupation.	Men Twenty Years and Upwards.				Increase Per Cent.
	1851.	Per 1000.	1881.	Per 1000.	
Railways	26,043	1·45	118,834	4·57	215
Carmen, Omnibus-men, &c.	79,546	4·44	145,939	5·61	27

There were twice the number of carmen, omnibus-men, cabmen, &c., in 1881 employed than there were thirty years before, though employment has been opened for nearly as many men in the railways of the Kingdom. And this is the experience as regards all kinds of machinery. They do not displace labour, but turn it to another channel.

Coachmen and cabmen have long hours. Omnibus-men in the metropolis work from eight in the morning till eleven at night. Omnibus drivers earn 6s. per day, conductors 4s. per day. The omnibus driver finds his own whip, and the conductor his lamp. Cabmen have an uncertain income. The practice in many cases is for cabowners to let their cabs to the cab drivers for a given term, who assume on themselves the risk of the day's fares. Carmen earn 18s. to 25s. per week, porters 18s. to 21s., horse-keepers 20s. to 24s., van-boys 7s. to 15s.; carmen's time average 13 hours, porters 11 hours, and horse-keepers 12 hours.

CARRIERS ON CANALS AND RIVERS: BARGEMEN, LIGHTERMEN, AND WATERMEN.

SUB-ORDER 3.

A WATERMAN is one who navigates, rows, or works for hire a passenger boat; a lighterman, or bargeman, one who navigates or works for hire a lighter, boat, or barge, conveying goods, wares, or merchandise.

The watermen and lightermen on the Thames form a company, incorporated by Act of Parliament, exercising the sole privilege over all parts of the river Thames as far as Gravesend; but beyond the Thames no such restriction obtains. Lightermen, watermen, and canal men earn good wages. Those on the Thames earn on an average fully 30s. a week. Those working elsewhere earn probably less.

This occupation is full of dangers. In many cases lightermen or bargemen work all night, and are exposed to night air and to the unhealthy exhalations of rivers and canals. They also work in small barges amidst large ships, and are met with on all sides by swift passing steamers. Whatever advantage they may have by working always in the open air, it is fully counterbalanced by the constant exposure to cold and wet.

SEAMEN.

SUB-ORDER 3.

THE Annual Return of Merchant Seamen gives the number of seamen employed in 1883 at 172,414 British, and 28,313 Foreign. In 1883 the number of apprentices enrolled was 2524, and on the 31st December, 1883, there were 11,449 Indentures in existence.

The wages of able seamen in sailing and steam vessels are given in the same return as follows, in the Ports of London and Liverpool, in the Return on Merchant Shipping (116) of 1884:—

MERCHANT SEAMEN.

	1850 Per month.	1860 Per month.	1870 Per month.		1880 Per month.		1883 Per month.	
			Sailing.	Steam.	Sailing.	Steam.	Sailing.	Steam.
LIVERPOOL—								
Mediterranean	50/-	50/-	50/-	60/-	50/-	55/-	60/-	65/-
North America	50/-	60/-	65/-	80/-	50/- to 60/-	70/- to 80/-	60/-	80/-
South America	45/-	50/-	50/-	60/-	50/-	55/- to 60/-	55/-	60/-
Coast of Africa	40/-	50/-	50/-	55/-	50/-	55/-	55/-	55/-
E. India & China	40/- to 45/-	50/-	50/-	55/-	50/-	55/-	55/-	60/-
Australia	45/-	50/-	50/-	55/-	50/-	—	55/-	60/-
LONDON—								
Mediterranean	45/-	50/-	60/- to 65/-	60/- to 70/-	50/- to 55/-	65/- to 75/-	60/-	65/- to 75/-
North America	50/-	55/- to 60/-	55/- to 70/-	70/- to 80/-	50/-	65/- to 70/-	60/-	75/- to 80/-
South America	45/-	50/-	50/-	60/- to 65/-	50/-	65/-	60/-	70/- to 75/-
Coast of Africa	45/-	50/-	50/-	—	50/- to 55/-	70/-	60/-	70/- to 75/-
E. India & China	40/-	50/-	50/-	60/- to 65/-	50/-	60/- to 65/-	60/-	70/- to 75/-
Australia	40/-	50/-	50/-	50/-	50/-	60/- to 65/-	60/-	70/- to 75/-

ESTIMATES OF THE EARNINGS

The average rates of wages paid per month to Engineers and Firemen on board vessels of the undermentioned tonnage were as follows:—

ENGINEERS' WAGES.

Year.	Vessels under 500 Tons.			500, and under 1000 Tons.				1000, and under 1500 Tons.			
	1st.	2nd.	Firemen.	1st.	2nd.	3rd.	Firemen.	1st.	2nd.	3rd.	Firemen.
	s. d.	s. d.	s. d.	s. d.	s. d.	s. d.	s. d.	s. d.	s. d.	s. d.	s. d.
1850	224 4	143 9	96 10	317 3	227 5	166 8	68 5	355 8	240 0	200 0	79 6
1860	213 3	160 0	98 11	240 8	191 8	153 9	77 0	348 8	246 0	198 8	86 6
1870	253 11	175 10	116 9	290 0	200 0	129 0	79 0	290 4	218 1	170 0	81 6
1880	268 11	184 10	117 0	311 10	216 0	156 9	71 11	326 0	234 0	163 0	73 11
1883	312 0	212 4	129 10	301 0	200 0	143 4	82 0	356 0	262 0	176 0	80 0

Year.	1500, and under 2000 Tons.				2000 Tons, and above.			
	1st.	2nd.	3rd.	Firemen.	1st.	2nd.	3rd.	Firemen.
	s. d.	s. d.	s. d.	s. d.	s. d.	s. d.	s. d.	s. d.
1850	345 10	261 3	214 7	80 11	447 9	276 3	225 5	81 10
1860	339 4	252 0	200 5	85 6	350 8	250 0	206 8	87 9
1870	330 0	241 0	197 0	79 8	372 0	289 0	224 0	85 1
1880	372 0	264 0	194 0	80 6	396 0	295 0	236 0	86 0
1883								

In the majority of cases the crews on board vessels under 500 tons find their own provisions, the averages under that tonnage are calculated on that scale.

A Return published by the Board of Trade of the lives lost by drowning or other accidents in British Merchant ships registered in the United Kingdom from the years 1871 to 1882 inclusive (C.—3875, 1884) gave the total number of crews lost at 35,660, and of passengers at 3062—total, 38,722. The yearly number of masters and crews lost by drowning were in the proportion of 1 in 80 in 1871, and 1 in 75 in 1882.

DOCK LABOURERS.

Sub-Order 3.

The following particulars have been kindly supplied by one of the London Dock Companies :—
In the warehouse staff—first-class leading foreman has 47s. 6d. to 50s. per week ; leading foreman, 40s. to 45s.; other foremen, 30s. to 40s.; coopers, 30s. to 40s. In the export staff—the assistant wharfinger, 30s. to 40s.; assistant measurer, 12s. to 20s.; piermen, 21s. to 30s. and uniform. In the dock-master's staff—masters of tugs, 30s. 9d. to 42s. 4d.; gatemen, 24s. to 27s. In the railway staff—platelayers, 21s. to 24s.; bridgemen, 21s. to 24s.; shunters, 18s. to 24s. In the engineer's staff—fitters, 42s. and a house; leading bricklayers, &c., 40s.; joiners, wheelwrights, &c., 42s.; engine drivers, 30s. to 35s.; stokers, 26s.; oilers, 26s. In the messengers' staff— head messenger, 40s. to 45s.; messengers, 5s. to 10s. and uniform. In the porter and labourer staff—shedmen, 24s. to 26s. and uniform; porters, 20s. to 25s.; first-class labourers, 30s.; second-class, 25s.; dock-house porters, 23s. and uniform.

WAREHOUSEMEN AND OTHERS ENGAGED IN STORAGE.

Sub-Order 4.

The wages of warehousemen are high. In Manchester many earn 30s. and 35s. a week. As an average, 25s. for men and 10s. for boys, 5s. for girls, and 10s. for women, may be considered rather below than above the usual earnings.

MESSENGERS AND PORTERS.

Sub-Order 5.

The wages of porters are low. In Liverpool the average wages of cotton porters for a considerable period has been 14s. a week; but there are gangs of men employed weekly who earn 21s., the captain earning 24s. Corn porters earn 11s. to 12s.; the captain of gangs, 24s. to 26s. In London few labourers can be had for less than 18s. to 20s.

CLASS IV.—AGRICULTURAL.

ORDER VII.

PERSONS WORKING THE LAND AND ENGAGED IN GROWING GRAIN, FRUITS, GRASSES, AND OTHER PRODUCTS.

AGRICULTURE—IN FIELDS AND PASTURE.

SUB-ORDER 1.

A CONSIDERABLE change has taken place in the system of Agriculture in the United Kingdom. Comparing the Agricultural Statistics of 1883 and 1866, we find that whilst the acreage in corn and green crops has diminished from 16,523,624 to 15,035,452 acres, the acreage in clover and permanent pasture increased from 26,499,834 to 31,660,319 acres. The number of cattle has increased from 8,569,693 in 1866 to 10,097,943 in 1883, but the number of sheep has diminished from 33,817,951 in 1867 to 28,347,560 in 1883. Meanwhile the importation of grain has greatly increased. The increase since 1840 has been as follows :—

	1840.	1860.	1880.	1883.
	Cwt.	Cwt.	Cwt.	Cwt.
Wheat..	8,637,993	25,484,151	55,261,924	64,138,631
Flour of wheat	1,537,838	5,086,220	10,558,312	16,329,312

And the average prices have been as follows :—

	1840.	1860.	1880.	1883.
	s. d.	s. d.	s. d.	s. d.
Wheat..	66 4	53 3	44 4	41 7
Barley..	36 5	36 7	33 1	31 10
Oats	25 8	24 5	23 1	21 5

The wages of agricultural labourers in England and Wales were given in Mr. Villiers' return for the year 1860, and its principal results were brought out in a paper on the subject read by Mr. Purdy of the Statistical Department of the Poor Law Board, at the Statistical Society.* From these documents it appeared that the average wages in the half year of 1860 were 11s. 7d. for men, and 4s. 2d. for women and children; the weekly earnings by task work being calculated at 13s. 9d. Basing his calculation upon Mr. Tufnell's report on Kent and Sussex, Mr. Purdy estimated the total earnings of agricultural labourers in England and Wales at £44 6s. 9d., or 17s. a week per family. The Earl of Shaftesbury, in a letter to the *Times*,† depicted the condition of Dorsetshire labourers in a very favourable manner; 14s. 6¼d. being calculated to be the average earning, each having a cottage either free or at a very small rent. Although the nominal wages might in some cases be as low as 8s. or 9s. per week in money, a free house and garden, fuel cut and dried, a chain of potato ground prepared and manured, and a bushel of wheat worth 5s. per month, raise the wages 4s. more per week, besides the gratuity given for extra work, and allowance for harvest work, &c. The wages in the different districts differed materially. In the northern and Yorkshire counties in immediate contiguity to the manufacturing districts the wages were higher than in the eastern, western, or midland counties; yet the force of public opinion and facility of communication tended to assimilate the wages throughout the country. The wages of agricultural labour increased as follows:—1824, 9s. 4d.; 1837, 10s. 4d.; 1860, 11s. 7d.; 1866, 13s.

In Scotland the wages, according to a similar return, moved for by Sir Andrew Agnew,‡ also commented upon in another paper by Mr. Purdy at the Statistical Society,|| were in 1860 as follows:—In the northern counties, men, 12s. 2¾d.; women, 5s. 1¾d.; children under 16, 4s. In the midland, men, 13s. 2d.; women, 5s. 7½d.; children, 4s. 0½d. In the southern, men, 13s. 2d.; women, 5s. 11½d.; children, 4s. 9½d.: giving an average for all Scotland at, men, 13s. 1d.; women, 5s. 7d.; children, 4s. 3¾d. The "North British Agriculturist" published from time to time during 1864 accounts of the wages of agricul-

* "Journal of the Statistical Society," vol. xxiv. p. 328. Return of the average rates of weekly earnings of agricultural labourers in the Unions of England and Wales (14 of 1861).

† See *Times*, January 29, 1866.

‡ 244 of 1861.

|| "Journal of the Statistical Society," vol. xxv. p. 425.

tural labour in distinct farms in the different counties in Scotland, which supported the above averages. The wages are paid half in money, half in food. £20 in cash is frequently given, but the allowances vary, some having house and garden, coal and meat, some the produce of a number of sheep or cows. The small crofters, at least 20,000 in number, cannot be taken to earn more on an average than 20s. a week for themselves and families.

The wages in Ireland were given in another return for 1860, moved for by Lord Dunkellin, and equally commented on by Mr. Purdy; and according to these the wages in 1860 averaged 7s. 1$\frac{1}{3}$d. for men, 3s. 11d. for women, and 2s. 11$\frac{1}{2}$d. for children.

The Reports of the Royal Commissioners on Agriculture in 1881-2 gave much information on the wages prevailing in the agricultural districts, and also of the cost of labour at different times, the substance of which is as follows:—Mr. Coleman's Report on Lancashire described the wages in 1851 at 11s. a week without extras; those in 1864 were 14s. a week, afterwards gradually increasing to 17s. a week with their breakfast every morning, and their turf carted, which made their wages equal to 19s. In Cheshire, day labourers earned 14s. per week, shepherds £1, carters 18s. Women were occasionally employed for weeding, pulling turnips, &c., at 7s. 6d. per week. In Northumberland the rate of wages ranged from 18s. a week in the locality of colliery and manufacturing enterprise, to 15s. in the purely agricultural districts, besides which the labourer has 1000 yards of potatoes, usually planted by the farmer, and worth from £3 10s. to £4, a cotter and coals 6d., which make a total wage of quite 18s. to 19s. a week. Mr. Bruce gave the wages in Bedfordshire at 12s. or 13s. a week for an ordinary labourer, 16s. to 18s. a week for carters, stockmen, and shepherds, higher wages prevailing in harvest and hay-time. The headmen on the farm are often provided with cottages and gardens, and in some instances with potato ground, rent free, women 1s. 6d. or 1s. a day. In Buckingham 13s. to 14s. per week in the winter, and 1s. to 2s. a week more in summer. Carters, cattle-men, and shepherds 1s. or 2s. more than ordinary labourers, and often have a cottage and garden rent free, and £2 or £3 extra at Michaelmas. In Cambridgeshire 12s. to 13s. per week for ordinary labourer with £4 10s. or £5 harvest-money; for carters, shepherds, stockmen, and horsemen about 15s., and in most cases a cottage and garden rent free. In Derby a tenant of the Duke of Devonshire paid £20 to £25 a year, and provided them with board. Ordinary labourers earn 2s. 6d. to 3s. per day. In Lincoln the usual wages were 18s. or £1 a week. Yearly labourers are paid in money, pork, flour, potatoes, cottage and garden rent free. The yearly married labourer receives 12s. to 14s. a week in money, with 30 stones of bacon per annum, and potatoes and money instead of beer in harvest and cottage and garden. The single labourers, who board with a foreman, receive in money £12 to £18 or £20 per annum and their board and lodging. In Middlesex labourers had 15s. to 16s. for ordinary men, and 24s. to 30s. for skilful men. In Norfolk 12s. to 18s. a week, harvest wages £1 10s. or £1 19s.; shepherds 15s. to 18s. a week. In Nottinghamshire, near the collieries, farm labourers get from 18s. to 21s. per week. Away from the collieries 13s. to 15s. per week for ordinary labourers, and 15s. to £1 per week for shepherds, waggoners, and headmen. In Somerset day labourers 12s., shepherd and carter 13s., cider and extra money in summer. In Devon 14s. to 15s., and women 10d. a day. In Dorset labourers 10s., carters and shepherds 12s. with harvest-money, liquor, full potato ground, cottage and garden.

In Ireland evidence was given before the Committee of the House of Commons on Agricultural Labourers (1884) that 8s. to 9s. a week was earned by labourers. In Limerick wages ranged from 9s. to 10s. a week.

The following comparative rates are likewise useful :—

HANTS.

—	Price of Mowing one acre of grass.	Price of Hoeing one acre of Turnips.	Price of Reaping one acre of Corn.
1861	—	—	10s. 6d. to 11s.
1865	—	5s. 9d.	10s. 11s.
1871	2s. 6d. 4s. 9d. 5s.	5s. 10s.	10s. 6d. to 13s.
1875	3s. 3d. 5s. 6d.	—	13s. 6d.
1880	4s. 7s. 6d.	5s. 6d. 11s.	13s. 15s.

NORTHUMBERLAND.

—	Foreman's wages ⅌ week.	Single Hand's wages ⅌ week.	Double Hands' wages ⅌ week.	Woman workers ordinary ⅌ day.	Women workers harvest ⅌ day.
	£ s. d.	£ s. d.	£ s. d.	s. d.	s. d.
1831	0 12 6	0 11 0	—	0 8	1 6
1835	0 12 6	0 10 6	—	0 8	1 6
1840	0 14 6	0 12 0	1 0 0	0 10	1 6
1845	0 14 6	—	0 18 0	0 10	1 6
1850	0 13 0	0 11 0	1 2 0	0 10	1 6
1855	0 16 0	0 14 0	1 7 0	0 10	1 6
1860	0 17 0	0 16 0	1 7 6	0 10	1 6
1865	0 18 0	0 15 0	1 8 0	0 10	1 6
1870	1 0 0	0 16 0	—	1 0	2 0
1875	1 4 0	1 4 0	—	1 4	3 0
1880	1 1 0	0 18 0	—	1 3	2 6

Agricultural labour is healthy. The relative rates of mortality in agricultural and manufacturing counties may be gathered from the following average for the ten years from 1872 to 1881:—

Agricultural Counties.	Rate of Mortality to 1000 living 1872—81	Manufacturing Counties.	Rate of Mortality to 1000 living 1872—81
Westmoreland	17·3	Chester	20·8
Bedford	19·0	Lancaster	24·8
Lincoln	18·3	Stafford	22·1
Wilts	18·3	Nottingham	21 3
Suffolk	19·5	West Riding, Yorkshire	23 0
Cambridge	18·4	Warwick	21·6

ORDER VIII.

PERSONS ENGAGED ABOUT ANIMALS.

FISHERMEN.*

SUB-ORDER 1.

THERE are in the United Kingdom about 120,000 persons constantly or occasionally employed in fishing, who, with their dependents, may be taken to represent upwards of 500,000 persons. And the total annual value of the British fisheries is estimated at £11,000,000, giving an average produce per head of about £22. In agricultural pursuits there are about 3,000,000 persons, and they raise annually produce to the value of about £270,000,000, giving an average of about £82 per head; that proportion being considerably exceeded in the manufacturing industry, which is so greatly aided by mechanical contrivances and the use of steam.

A considerable amount of capital is invested in the British fisheries. Assuming £10 per ton as the value of the fishing boats, exclusive of the large ships employed in the whale and sea fisheries, and others, £10 per ton for gear, nets, &c., the 350,000 tons employed in fisheries would represent £7,000,000, while £3,000,000 more may be taken as the capital invested in all the processes of curing, preserving, &c., making in all £10,000,000 capital employed in the fisheries of the United Kingdom, in the proportion of three-fourths fixed and one-fourth floating. The number of men and boys constantly employed in fishing, resident

* See Notes on the Sea Fisheries and Fishing Population of the United Kingdom by Vice-Admiral H.R.H. the Duke of Edinburgh, and my Paper on the Economic Condition of Fishermen read at the Conferences in connection with the great International Fisheries Exhibition (1883).

within the limits of the ports, was reported to the Fishery Exhibition at 69,073, and the number of persons other than regular fishermen occasionally employed in fishing at 59,279, making a total of 128,372.

The conditions under which fishermen pursue their calling differ considerably in the fishing ports. In Hull, the custom is to divide the proceeds by eighths, according to the scale, by averages; the skipper taking so many, the mate so many, and the men so many, they again paying for their provisions in similar proportions. At Lowestoft the general practice is for fishermen to be joint adventurers with the owner. The owner gives the boat, gear, and net, the fishermen give their labour. At the end of the fishing the accounts are settled. Out of the gross proceeds the expenses of the boat, food of fishermen, salt, commission, &c., are first deducted, and of the net proceeds the half goes to the owner, a share is taken for the boat, a half share for the net, and the remainder is divided among the master and fishermen, according to their position in the boat. At Yarmouth the proceeds are divided into six parts, and each participates in so many sixths. In some parts of Ireland the owner of the boat takes half, keeps the boat in repair, and supplies the net, the other half being divided among the men in equal shares. In Scotland, the curers engage fishermen at a fixed price per cran of herrings, and pay them £10, £20, or £30, as the case may be, as bounty, the advance constituting a debt against the fishermen. This method is specially noticed by Mr. Bertram as decidedly objectionable. The bargain, it appears, is, that the curer will take, say, two hundred crans of herrings certain, and pay for them at so much per cran to a boat-owner, giving him an advance on the same. The boat-owner again, on his side, has to provide the boat, nets, buoys, and all the apparatus of the fishery, and he engages a crew to fish, usually hired men, who get so much wages at the end of the season, and have no risk or profit. The bargain is made at one season for another; so that, in anticipation of the result, the curer pays the bounty and makes the necessary preparations in providing barrels, salt, and other necessaries for the cure, and the boat-owner receives his pay, one year in advance, for next year's work. In the same manner curers will advance money to young fishermen, in order that they may purchase a boat and the necessary quantity of netting.

A much better system prevails in the whale and seal fisheries. There the crews are paid partly by wages and partly by a share of the catch, in the shape of oil money, or skin money. The captain receives, say, £5 per month, 5s. per ton oil money,

10s. 6d. per ton whalebone, and the mate £2 15s. per month and proportionate allowances, and so every other officer and man in proportion. There are, therefore, three systems more or less prevalent, viz., that of partnership of profit and loss; that of master and labourer, or a payment by wages pure and simple; and that of labour and wages, with the addition of a percentage on the produce of the fishery.

What is the present amount of earnings of fishermen it is difficult to estimate. Where they are paid by fixed wages the rates are usually 15s. and even 20s. a week, but such wages can only be reckoned upon for a few months in the year. Where fishermen share in the profits, the income varies considerably. In all cases, nine months' labour is the most that the fisheries afford, whilst those not constantly but occasionally employed in fishing must reckon upon still less employment; and, though there is something to do in connection with the fisheries for women and children, the earnings of these are usually very slender. From information received,* I find that a crew of seal and whale fishing, consisting of fifty-one men besides the captain, received on average £2 18s. per month, besides the percentage on oil, skins, &c. For nine months their earnings would be £26 for each man. In the Report of the Committee appointed to inquire into the Sea Fishing Trade, there is an account of a settlement or fishing voyage in 1881. Out of a gross produce of £551, and a net stock of £397, the people's part, divided in shares, was £174, or £18 15s. 6d. each. From various accounts which I had the opportunity of examining, the net share falling on the fishermen may be taken at 30 per cent. of the total gross amount. To this sum, however, there must be added the cost of the food of fishermen whilst engaged in fishing, but we must deduct from the amount the portion of loss for gear and net charged on them, as well as the cost of the fishermen's dress and equipment. In plain figures, the account may approximately be put down as follows:—

	£
30 per cent. to fishermen of £11,000,000 gross produce ...	3,300,000
Food of fishermen, 80,000 for 9 months at 8s. a week, say £16 each	1,000,000
	4,300,000
Deduct 10 per cent. for share of loss of gear, clothing, &c.	500,000
	£3,800,000

* See Documents in Appendix B. kindly supplied by Messrs. Walter, Greeve, Son, &c., of Greenock, Messrs. W. O. Taylor, &c., Dundee Polar Fishery Company, Dundee, and M. David Tray, of Peterhead. Practical information has also been received by the Shetland fishermen through Captain Bain.

Divide this amount by 120,000, and we have an average of £31 13s. per annum each, or 12s. per week. But the £1,000,000 calculated as the cost of the fisherman's board does not come home to the family. The share really falling to the fisherman's family, to support four or five persons, is £3,300,000, less £500,000, or £2,800,000, or £23 per family, or about 9s. per week. To this, doubtless, there must be added any supplementary income from other sources. A small croft, an occasional employment in a ship as sailor, the allowance from the Naval Reserve, where it can be had, all help, only such extra income is very uncertain; it is not shared in by all fisherfolk, and, in any case, it is small, and cannot essentially alter the economic condition of our fishermen.

The great danger of life with fishermen is from wreck. In 1865, 98 fishing smacks were wrecked, but many isolated accidents occur of which we have no account. The Royal National Lifeboat Institution and the Shipwrecked Mariners' Society—the one to save life and the other to assist and relieve all wrecked seamen—are conferring an immense benefit on the seafaring classes of the United Kingdom.*

HORSE-KEEPERS, GAME-KEEPERS, AND DROVERS.

Sub-Order 2.

AMONG these are horse-keepers, game-keepers, drovers, and others engaged in minor occupations.

The earnings of these classes of persons vary very much. The wages of horse-keepers are 21s. in London, and 15s. to 18s. in the country. Game-keepers and drovers earn 12s. to 16s. each per week.

---

* The Royal National Lifeboat Institution has 162 lifeboats, and by them and other special exertions it is enabled to save from 600 to 700 lives in a year. In 1866 the Lifeboat Institution has been the means of saving 921 lives. The Shipwrecked Mariners' Society has been instituted for three objects :—1st. To board, lodge, clothe, and forward to their homes, or to their nearest Consuls, if foreigners, all wrecked seamen or other poor persons of all nations. 2nd. To assist seamen to replace their clothes, boats, &c., when lost by storms or other accidents of the sea, and to relieve their widows ; and 3rd. To give gold and silver medals or other pecuniary rewards for any praiseworthy endeavour to save life from shipwreck. Other institutions of great benefit to seamen are: the British and Foreign Sailors' Society, the Sailors' Homes, and the recently-established Belvidere Institution and Mariners' National Pension and Widows' Fund.

CLASS V.—INDUSTRIAL.

ORDER IX.
PERSONS WORKING IN BOOKS, PRINTS, AND MAPS.

PRINTERS.

SUB-ORDER 1.

PRINTERS are found in every part of the United Kingdom, but it is in London and Edinburgh that the bulk of the printing is carried on.

The labour of printers is divided between compositors, readers, pressmen, and machinemen. An apprenticeship of seven years is required to become a journeyman printer, except that the eldest son of a printer has a right by patrimony to become a journeyman without indenture.

Among printers there are offices with day work only, and offices where night work is always going on, and offices with a mixed work. Those who work in the day commence at eight or nine in the morning and end at seven to eight in the evening, Saturdays being from eight to two p.m. Those who work at night commence at five p.m. and end between three and five a.m. In some offices Sunday labour is performed, especially newspaper work.

The average earnings in a large printing-office in the metropolis for the year was—compositors, £103 14s.; readers, £138 4s.; machine minders and engineers, £111 15s.; warehousemen, £82; pressmen, £84; boys, 9s. 6d., per week, in all cases including overtime. The wages in another large house averaged as follows—compositors, 33s. 3d.; pressmen, 30s.; machinemen, 31s.; readers, 43s. 5d. In morning newspaper offices the earnings of a compositor vary from 50s. to 70s. per week, or even 80s. In a printing office some are paid by the piece, others are on the establishment. Those on the establishment in book houses cannot receive less than 36s. Those paid by the piece earn according as they are regularly employed, as they are quick in composition, make fewer errors, and have more or less remunerative kind of work. In Edinburgh, the wages are—compositors, settled wages, 26s.; piecemen, 20s., pressmen, settled, 26s.; machinemen, 27s. to 30s. Apprentice compositors, 7s. to 10s.; machinemen, 9s. to 15s. Establishment wages vary in different towns from 21s. to 30s. per week. On an average, the wages may be taken at 30s. for men; 10s. boys; 12s., women; girls, 8s.

The London Society of Compositors gave the following particulars:—

Journeymen compositors are paid a minimum wage of 36s. per week, but numbers receive 38s., 40s., and so on, both in book and weekly newspaper offices. Daily newspapers are in all cases produced by piece hands, by whom all composition is done, no apprentices being employed on either morning or evening papers. Apprentices in book and weekly newspaper offices receive in most cases two-thirds of their earnings, although some are employed at a weekly wage, increasing each year. Women are only employed as compositors in one or two non-society offices in London, having invariably proved a failure in our business, although no objection to their employment is made by us, provided they are paid in accordance with the scale and customs of the trade. The term of apprenticeship in all branches of the printing business in London is seven years —14 to 21, at which age adult wages begin.

It is difficult to give anything like reliable data, but the average of a daily news hand may be taken at 50s. per week, a weekly news hand 40s. per week, and a book hand 30s. per week.

The number of members employed on daily papers is about 600, about 5600 being employed on weekly newspapers and book-work. No overtime is paid on daily papers, 3d. per hour extra being paid to establishment hands on weekly papers after the ordinary working hours, and to piece hands after they have worked six hours of overtime, but in all cases after twelve o'clock. Piece hands on book-work are also paid 3d. per hour extra for all time worked after the ordinary working hours.

There are no fixed hours for daily news hands, but weekly news and book hands work 54 hours—9½ the first five days, and 6 hours on Saturdays.

In nearly all the daily newspaper offices the compositors receive a week or a fortnight's holiday each year, with an average of their earnings at the expense of the proprietors, the time varying according to length of servitude. The same boon exists, also, in a *few* of the other printing offices.

All tools belong to the compositors themselves.

Compositors' wages have undergone very little change, the book hands' wages being increased in 1810, 1847, 1866, and 1872. In 1866 a halfpenny per 1000 was added to the piece prices, and the establishment wages increased from 33s. for 63 hours to 36s. for 60 hours, while in 1872 an additional halfpenny was added to the piece rate and the hours reduced to 54.

The Amalgamated Association of Pressmen report as follows :—

Our trade is one that has to a large extent been superseded by machinery, though there is still sufficient demand for the few competent men who remain in or are brought up to it. The wages for time hands is 36s. per week of 54 hours, working 9½ hours on five days to make up for the short day on Saturday. Overtime is paid 3d. per hour extra—*i.e.*, 11d. per hour. No tools are found by the workman, neither is there any deduction from wages. Apprenticeship is for seven years. Piece-work predominates, the prices being based on the possibility of two men of average capacity (for we work as a rule in pairs) earning 6s. per day of nine hours. On these piece prices earnings vary considerably, according to the age, energy, or capacity of the men, so that in some cases, on the same description of work, the earnings of two presses (four men) vary sometimes as much as £1 per week. It is therefore difficult to state an average for the whole trade, but as near as can be judged the earnings of a competent piece hand would average about 32s. per week in ordinary years.

The only change in the rate of wages during the last fifty years or more was in 1866, up to which time there had been two recognised prices for time hands—one of 33s. per week, the other of 36s. The latter was, in that year, made the minimum. Piece prices have in most cases risen in proportion.

Although there has been but little change in wages, the number of working hours has been twice reduced. In 1866, contemporaneously with the rise of wages, the hours were reduced from 63 to 60, and again in 1872 to 54, the present number.

There is a considerable section of our trade who from age or other incapacitating circumstances is unemployed for a great part of the year. An average which should include this class would be as misleading as the enumerations of sick and disabled in the strength of an army. If trade is bad this section is swollen by the accession of many who in prosperous times are fully employed. Perhaps the best index to the prosperity of a trade is the number of recipients of unemployed pay. In our case the percentage varies from 20 to 37; the latter being reached in 1879, the worst year we have known. In bad times we have as many as 17 per cent. of the members signing the out-of-work book at one time. This is probably a greater percentage of unemployed than can be shown by any other trade. Our position in this respect is analogous to that of a small benefit society which finds its numbers stationary or declining while its liabilities are increasing. But the principal cause of the precariousness of employment is that machinery is kept going in preference to piece-workers, even if the latter can produce the work at a cheaper rate; so that they are the first to feel any fluctuation in the trade.

A full half among the intelligent and steady printers are householders, living in houses at the rental of £25 to £35 per annum in the metropolis, though they often sublet part of the house.

BOOKBINDERS AND BOOKFOLDERS.

SUB-ORDER 1.

THE work of bookbinders is generally divided into forwarding and finishing: forwarding, being the acutal binding of the book, includes that part of bookbinding which consists in putting a book together, cutting and gilding or colouring the pages, and covering it with leather; finishing, being the ornamenting of the book, includes lettering of the title of the book on the back, decorating the book, or working patterns in different coloured leather on the book.

The hours of labour are generally from eight to eight, except on magazine days, when a good deal of overtime becomes necessary.* Full time generally lasts from the beginning of September to the end of February, but sometimes extends longer, and at others falls short.

The wages are generally paid by piece-work, the earnings depending on the quantity of work performed. In London the piece-worker will earn as much as 38s. to 76s. a week; the time-worker from 32s. to 40s., the actual earnings being from 20s. to 25s. in slack times, up to 40s. when fully employed; the finisher, 45s.; the forwarder, 45s.; and women from 12s. to 18s. Much depends also on the kind of work and the time of the year. In Edinburgh the wages are given at: men, time-

---

* See Report on Bookbinders in the Fifth Report of the Children's Employment Commission, 1862.

workers, 20s. to 26s.; girls, 8s. to 10s.; piece-workers, 25s. to 35s.; girls, 9s. to 14s. Apprentice boys, 5s. 6d. to 18s.; girls, 2s. 6d. to 7s.

The bookbinder requires no tools of any value.

LITHOGRAPHERS..

Sub-Order 2.

THIS industry requires labour even more skilful than that wanted for printing, and those engaging in it receive a large income.

The wages in an important establishment in London are given as follows :—Artist, £3 to £4 per week; writers, £2 10s. to £3; journeymen printers, stationers, &c., £2 to £2 15s.

Order X.

PERSONS WORKING AND DEALING IN MACHINES AND IMPLEMENTS.

MACHINE TOOLS AND IMPLEMENT MAKERS.

Sub-Order 1.

WAGES vary in the engineering trade from 28s. per week in some parts of Yorkshire to 36s. and 38s. in London, but they average 31s. 6d. in the United Kingdom. The rule is to pay by the week of 54 hours. Apprentices are paid generally 3s. per week when starting at 14 years of age, and advancing one shilling per week till they are 21, when they are paid from 4s. to 6s. less than the ordinary tradesman for one or two years after they become journeymen. Piecework exists in locomotive and machine works, but is not general in stationary engine works. Many men work by what is called "the piece," but only draw day wages. The highest premium on piecework is a third extra to the day wages earned.

Foremen are paid according to agreement with their employers, varying from £2 to £3 per week. Overtime is paid for extra to the 54 hours, in some cases time and a quarter, time and a half, and Sunday double time.

Machinery and tools are found by the employers, except in the case of the pattern makers, who find saws, edged tools, &c., which is equal to one shilling per week off their earnings.

In some districts holidays are more numerous than others, but independently of slack times men work 50 weeks in each year, the other two weeks being forced holidays, such as Christmas, Easter, Whitsuntide, and Bank Holidays.

Wages in Lancashire which in 1850 were about 30s. per week, at the same towns are now 32s. In the North of England they were about 26s. in 1850, now they run from 30s. to 33s. for 54 hours. Speaking broadly, engineers' wages have advanced about 3s. all round (per week) within the past 30 years, whilst hours have been reduced from three to five hours per week in the same period.

Mr. Robinson, of Messrs. Sharp, Stuart, and Co., kindly favoured the following comparative rates of wages at the Atlas Works, Manchester:—

	1851		1864		1874	1884
	Rates	Averages	Rates	Averages	Rates	Rates
Fitters & Erectors	26/- to 35/-	30·18	26/- to 34/-	30·24	32/- to 38/-	32/- to 38/-
Turners & Borers	—	—	—	—	32/- ,, 35/-	—
Grinders	28/- ,, 32/-	29·40	30/-	30·	33/-	32/-
Joiners	26/- ,, 30/-	26·36	27/- to 30/-	28·90	30/- to 32/-	32/-
*Pattern Makers	30/- ,, 32/-	30·50	28/- ,, 31/-	31·50	30/- ,, 36/-	36/-
*Painters	23/- ,, 28/-	20·25	26/- ,, 29/-	26·42	26/- ,, 32/-	30/-
Coppersmiths	None	—	30/- ,, 32/-	31·20	—	—
Planers, Slotters, and Shapers	18/- to 21/-	19·87	16/- ,, 28/-	21·72	18/- ,, 28/-	22/- to 27/-
Brass Moulders	Piecework	—	32/-	32·	32/-	34/-
Iron Moulders	,,	—	28/- to 36/-	33·54	36/-	36/-
Angle Iron Smiths	36/-	36·	38/-	38·	40/-	38/-
Platers	28/- to 31/-	29·06	36/-	36·	38/-	36/-
Rivetters	26/- ,, 27/-	26·06	30/- to 31/-	31·	34/-	32/-
Holders-up	23/-	23·	26/- ,, 29/-	28·75	31/-	29/-
Helpers	18/- to 21/-	19·50	18/- ,, 19/-	18·22	19/-	19.-
Smiths	26/- ,, 36/-	30·27	26/- ,, 42/-	31·38	30/- to 45/-	32/-
Strikers	18/- ,, 21/-	18·45	18/- ,, 22/-	19·06	20/- ,, 24/-	20/-

At those works the wages of apprentices begin at 4s. per week, and are advanced to a maximum of 15s. per week. Adult wages commence at the age of 21 years. The percentage of piece-work earnings over the weekly rates in each class of workmen cannot be given separately, but the average for the last twelve months of all classes was 18·6 per cent.

Foremen are in every case excluded from the rates enclosed. They are paid a weekly rate of wages, and receive a bonus on the turn-out of work from their respective shops.

* The class of men who are marked thus (*) are the only classes who are not on piecework here. The piecework earnings, in addition to the wages given above, are from 20 to 50 per cent.

Labourers are paid by the hour, not by the piece. In the case of a gang of men and boys working on one job they are paid in proportion to the number of hours each has worked, and also to the weekly rate of wages of each during the month for which the piece-work accounts are being settled for.

Overtime is in all cases paid far at the rate of $1\frac{1}{4}$ time rate for the first two hours, and at $1\frac{1}{2}$ time rate after that, the piece-work price remaining unchanged.

All classes of men work the whole year except one week at the New Year, one week at Whitsuntide, three days at Easter, Christmas-day, and August Bank Holiday.

Of course, in case of slackness of work every man is liable to be dismissed or suspended for a time.

The last variation in wages took place in this district in March, 1881, when all men receiving 28s. per week and upwards had their wages raised 2s. per week, and all paid less than 28s. were raised 1s. per week. This restored the rates to those paid previous to December, 1878, except in the case of boiler makers, who had been then reduced 4s. per week all round.

CUTLERY.

Sub-Order 2.

Sheffield is the centre of the cutlery manufacture as Birmingham is of the hardware. The other localities of importance are Ecclesall Bierlow and Wortley.

In most of the trades of Sheffield a full seven years' apprenticeship is required. The work is carried on partly in factories, but extensively also in private houses and workshops.

The hours of labour in workshops and private houses are very irregular.

The labourer must purchase tools which are often very expensive, or, if he has the use of them from his master, the rent of them is deducted from his wages.

The wages vary very much, even with the equally skilled. There are men who can earn 35s. per week, and men on precisely the same class of goods who cannot earn 20s. Some men can get the work quickly out of hand, whilst others cannot get rid of it, and all have served the same length of time to it, and are quite as good workmen. Workers are mostly paid by the piece, but some few are paid by the day. The men earn, by day, from 28s. to 35s. per week; the women, 8s., 10s., 12s., and 16s.; girls over fourteen, 3s. 6d. to 6s. The average earnings for the last six months have been about 20s. for slow men, as described above, and 28s.

for the quicker men. The ordinary number of hours is 54 hours per week, but the men do not attend at regular hours. Skilled men will not. Not half of the men are at work at nine o'clock. The men work all the year except Christmas week, three days at Whitsuntide, and two days at Easter and Bank Holiday.

WATCHMAKERS.

Sub-Order 3.

The watch manufacture is divided into a large number of departments. There are finishers, motioners, jewellers, engravers, gilders, springers, case makers, cap makers, hand makers, index makers, pallet makers, balance makers, dial makers, pendant makers, glass makers, escapement makers, movement makers, engine turners, joint finishers, and fuzee cutters.* Few watches are now made in England.

Present wages are given—Clockmakers, 23s., 25s., 28s., 30s., 42s.; average, 29s. Watchmakers, 30s., 40s., 50s., 60s., and 85s.; average, 35s.

PHILOSOPHICAL INSTRUMENT MAKERS, OPTICIANS, SCALE MAKERS, AND SURGICAL INSTRUMENT MAKERS.

Sub-Order 3.

This work, which is highly skilled, is carried on partly in shops and partly in private houses. The workman has little or no expense in tools.

The wages, mostly all by piece-work, are seldom as low as 20s. to 25s., and are often 50s. and 70s.; for the whole number, 35s. for men, and 12s. for those under 20 may be taken.

MUSICAL INSTRUMENT MAKERS.

Sub-Order 6.

The wages of pianoforte makers and other instrument makers range from 30s. to 50s. and 60s. per week; on an average, they may be taken at 33s. for men, and 12s. under 20.

* See " Birmingham and the Midland Hardware Trade," p. 195.

The manufacture of musical instruments does not seem injurious to health :—

Occupation.	Ages.			
	25	35	45	55
All Classes	·985	1·305	1·853	3·215
Musical Instrument Makers ..	·731	1·299	1·876	2·831

ORDER XI.
PERSONS WORKING IN HOUSES, FURNITURE, AND DECORATIONS.

BUILDERS.

SUB-ORDER 1.

IN 1868 the current rates of wages for workmen were as follows : — Bricklayers, masons, carpenters, joiners, slaters, plasterers, 8d. per hour for 56½ hours per week—viz., 6½ Saturday, 10 Monday, 10 Tuesday, 10 Wednesday, 10 Thursday, 10 Friday, making £1 17s. 8d. per week. Plumbers, 9d. per hour for 47 hours per week—viz., 4½ Saturday, 8½ Monday, 8½ Tuesday, 8½ Wednesday, 8½ Thursday, 8½ Friday, making £1 15s. 3d. per week. Painters and glaziers, 7d. to 7¼d. per hour for 56½ hours per week. Labourers average 5d. per hour. Full time 56½ hours, as above, but overtime often made.

After three months' strike, on August 29th, 1872, wages were increased ½d. per hour, and the hours of work reduced from 56½ to 52½ hours—viz., 6½ Saturday, 10 . Monday, 10 Tuesday, 10 Wednesday, 10 Thursday, 10 Friday, equal 56½, to 5½ Saturday, 9 Monday, 9½ Tuesday, 9½ Wednesday, 9½ Thursday, 9½ Friday, equal 52½ hours.

On August 2nd, 1873, in consequence of the briskness of trade, wages were again increased ½d. per hour, the hours of work remaining unchanged. This was agreed to after several meetings of the delegates of masters and men without strike.

These rates of wages still remain the same, of which the following is a detailed statement.

The following are the recognised rates at present, but more or less are in some cases paid, according to the working abilities of the men, the details of which it would be impossible to give:—

	Total Hours.	Rate.	Wages.	1st hour overtime.	2nd hour overtime.	Until midnight, five days per week.	Saturday afternoon, Sunday, and after midnight.
Bricklayers	52½	9	£1 19 4½	1d. extra	2d. extra	Time & half	Double time
Masons	,,	,,	,,	,,	,,	,,	,,
Carpenters	,,	,,	,,	,,	,,	,,	,,
Joiners	,,	,,	,,	,,	,,	,,	,,
Slaters	,,	,,	,,	,,	,,	,,	,,
Plasterers	,,	,,	,,	,,	,,	,,	,,
Mason Fixer	¾d. per hour over above rates.						
Staircase Hand (joiner)	1d. ,, ,, ,, ,, (average).						
Plumbers	47	10	1 19 2	Time and quarter		Do. 6 days do. Time & half	Do. not Sat. aft. Double time
,, Labourers	47	6	1 3 6	,,		,,	,,
Glaziers	52½. From 8d. to 8½d. Various rates for overtime.						
Painters	6d. per hour (average), 52½ are full time, but extra hours are often made. No extra money for overtime is as a rule paid.						
Labourers							

N.B.—No extra money for overtime in any trade if worked by request of men.

On July 28th, 1877, the masons of London went out on

OF THE WORKING CLASSES. 107

strike for 10d. per hour (an increase of 1d. per hour) and 5½ hours less time (to commence at 7 o'clock each day—1 hour in 5 days and ½ hour on Monday, equals 5½ hours), but after 32 weeks' strike, and having failed in their object, work was resumed on March 14th, 1878, at the old time and rates.

Mr. Lord, in his valuable tables of wages in Manchester, gave the comparative rates of builders as follows :—

TABLE X.
BUILDING.

Description.	Wages Earned Weekly in				
	1850. s. d.	1860. s. d.	1870. s. d.	1877. s. d.	1883. s. d.
Joiners	24 0	26s. to 28s.	32 0	38 7	36 4
,, Labourers ..	17 0	17 0	18 0	21 8	22 8¾
Bricklayers ..	26 0	30 0	32 0	43 1½	38 7
,, Labourers ..	17 0	18 0	20 5	23 10	25 0
Masons	24 0	27 0	30 0	37 1½	32 8
,, Labourers ..	17 0	18 0	20 5	22 8	20 5
Plasterers ..	26 0	28 0	32 0	38 0	36 4
,, Labourers ..	17 0	20 0	22 0	24 0	22 9
Percentage increase on 1850..	..	10·12	23·11	48·21	39·76

CABINET MAKERS AND UPHOLSTERERS.

Sub-Order 2.

UNDER this sub-order are included cabinet makers and upholsterers, undertakers, chair makers, picture-frame makers, polishers, carvers and gilders, bedstead, mattress, and bed tick makers.

Bed and mattress makers earn by the piece, 30s.; sewing women, 11s.; horse-hair curlers, 40s. to 45s., out of which they pay a boy 4s. to 5s. a week; women sorting hair and feathers earn 6s. to 10s.; cabinet makers, 7d. to 9d. per hour, sometimes they earn 50s. to 60s.; chair and sofa makers, 35s.; carvers and gilders, 34s.; upholsterers, 40s. to 50s.; French polishers, 8d. per hour.

Cabinet makers work 54 to 60 hours per week; chair makers, 60 hours; carvers and gilders, 54 to 57 hours; French polishers, 54 hours; upholsterers, 57 hours; horse-hair curlers, 60 hours.

The workman must provide himself with tools, which are costly.

Cabinet Makers.—When paid by time 9d. an hour given. When piece-work the average earnings may be taken at £2 a week. Highly skilled labour £2 10s. Overtime unusual. Foreman receives £3 10s. a week. Workmen find their own tools, the outlay, say, of £20 to £30. Employment tolerably constant.

Upholsterers.—Indoor and outdoor work; 9d. per hour men, 3d. per hour women. For indoor work, average wages earned by men £2 5s. to £2 10s. a week; for outdoor work (about a month in the year), 36s. to £2 a week. Women average about 15s. a week; apprentices, from 3s. to 18s. a week. Indoor piece-work, £2 5s. to £2 10s. a week. Hours, 8.30 a.m. to 7 p.m. (less an hour for dinner), 4½ hours on Saturdays—54 hours a week. Supply own tools (few required). Employment constant.

Painters.—Time-work. Average wages, 8¼d. per hour; skilled, 9d. per hour. Labourers, 6d. to 6¼d. per hour. Fifty-three and a half hours full time—from 6.30 a.m. to 5.30 p.m. Overtime wages, 8¼d. up to eight o'clock p.m.; after eight, 1s. 1¼d.; 12 p.m. to 6 a.m., 1s. 5d. Tools, &c., supplied. Employment not constant. Say nine months out of twelve.

Gilders.—All time-work. Average wages, 8¼d. per hour. Fifty-eight hours worked per week—7 a.m. to 7 p.m., and 7 a.m. to 1 p.m. on Saturdays. All tools, &c., supplied. Employment, nine months out of twelve; average earnings, 35s. a week. Wages have risen ½d. an hour since 1870.

Chairmakers.—The labour is skilled in this. Average wages, £2 a week.

Polishers.—Time-work; wages, 7d. to 8½d. per hour; hours, 7 a.m. to 7 p.m.; 7 a.m. to 1 p.m. on Saturdays; overtime, rare; 58 hours a week worked. Tools supplied. Employment, say, ten months out of twelve at least.

Carvers.—Mostly time-work. Wages vary very much, according to skill—from 9d. to 15d. per hour. Time, 52½ hours, a week—from 8 a.m. to 7 p.m., and 8 a.m. to 1 p.m. on Saturdays. Workmen supply their own tools; outlay small, say £6. Employment fairly constant.

	1839		1849		1859		1881	
	s	d	s.	d.	s.	d.	s.	d.
Cabinet and Chair Makers	26	0	28	0	28	0	30	6
Carvers	45	0	30	0	30	0	31	0
Polishers	17	0	20	0	20	0	30	10½
Upholsterers	27	0	30	0	30	0	32	0

WOOD CARVERS AND TOY MAKERS.

SUB-ORDER 3.

THE wages in these occupations are usually high, since they require consummate skill and precision. On an average, they are 35s. men; 12s. boys under 20; 14s. women, and 8s. girls.

ORDER XII.

PERSONS WORKING IN CARRIAGES AND HARNESS.

COACH MAKERS.

SUB-ORDER 11.

THE Miscellaneous Statistics for 1866 gave the wages in Edinburgh as follows:—Smiths, 1st class, 27s.; 2nd class, 22s.; vicemen, 1st class, 18s.; 2nd class, 16s.; 3rd class, 14s.; body makers, 1st class, 30s.; 2nd class, 22s.; carriage makers, 23s.;

painters, 22s. and 20s.; trimmers, 1st class, 25s.; 2nd class, 20s.; 3rd class, 18s.; wheelwrights, 22s.; 2nd class, 18s.; spring makers, 26s.; strikers, 18s.; labourers, 14s. In Liverpool, carriage makers, 30s.; body makers, 30s.; trimmers, 32s. In London the wages range from 25s. to 40s.

Present wages are—Body makers, 40s.; carriage makers, 46s.; smiths, 40s.; hammermen, 17s.; vicemen, 24s.; painters, 27s.; trimmers, 29s.; budget trimmers, 24s.; wheelers, 31s.; platers, 30s.; sawyers, 33s.; helpers, 18s.

Order XIII.

PERSONS WORKING IN SHIPS AND BOATS.

SHIPBUILDERS, SHIPWRIGHTS.

Sub-Order 1.

The tonnage of vessels built in the United Kingdom has greatly increased in recent years. The average yearly tonnage built since 1859 has been as follows:—

	Tons.
1859—1863	240,980
1864—1868	354,950
1869—1873	342,997
1874—1878	432,802
1879—1883	539,542

The tonnage built in 1883 reached 768,573 tons, but there has been a reaction since.

The wages are stated to be—Platers, 36s.; drillers, 25s.; rivetters, 34s.; ship carpenters, 34s.; joiners, 33s. 6d.; saw miller, 31s. On the Clyde—boiler makers earned 9d. per hour; caulkers, 9d.; platers, 10d.; ship plumbers, 8½d.; engineers, 7d. to 8d. per hour. A caulker by piece-work earned £2 11s. 9d., a rivetter £4 10s., and a fitter £5 5s. to £7 6s. 3d. per week speak of the average time and wages earned in a shipbuilding yard.

Order XIV.

Persons Working in Chemicals and Compounds.

CHEMICAL.

Sub-Order 3.

In 1866 the wages in Newcastle were as follows:—Foremen, 5s. 4d. per day; time-keepers, 3s. 4d.; engine men, 3s. 10d.; foremen, boiler men, 3s. 8d.; sulphuric acid makers, 4s. 6d.; sulphate of soda makers, 4s. 8d.; crude soda, 4s. 6d.; carbonate of soda makers, 4s. 6d.; crystals of soda, 3s. 8d.; bicarbonate of soda, 3s. 8d.; bleaching powder makers, 5s. 2d.; lads and boys, 1s. 6d. to 2s. a day. In Bristol the wages are the same; in Glasgow, something less. On an average, the wages may be taken at 22s. for men; 8s. boys; 6s. girls, and 8s. women.

Present wages are given as follows:—
Chemical works:—Alkali furnacemen, 25s. 6d.; labourers, 15s.; vitriol men, 28s.; labourers, 18s.; sulphate men, 23s. 6d.; labourers, 17s.; coopers, 30s.; bleaching powder makers, 25s. 8d.; labourers, 16s.; joiners, 34s. 4d.; pattern makers, 30s.; carters, 20s. 6d.

Mechanics and labourers work 54 hours per week, or 9 hours per day of six days. Burnermen are on 8 hours' shifts, but all the other pressmen 13 hours.

Order XV.

Persons Working in Tobacco and Pipes.

In tobacco and cigar factories journeymen make, by piecework, 30s. to 40s. per week; journeywomen, 14s. to 15s.; girls, 6s. to 10s.

Order XVI.

Persons working in food and spirituous drinks.

Malting and Brewing.

Sub-Order 2.

In malting two per cent. of the workers are foremen; workmen are employed each day on an average 11 hours, exclusive of meals' time, and they earn 38s. per week. Ten per cent. are firemen; their work is, in winter, 13 hours and in summer 9 hours, and their earnings 25s. per week. Twenty-five per cent. are floormen and they earn 24s. 4d. per week. Sixty-three per cent. are ordinary maltsters, and labourers who may be taken to earn 4d. an hour. In the work of preparation and delivery of malt a week is 54 hours. In the work of making malt a week is 73½ hours. This season extends over 7 months. There is, in all cases, given a quart of ale and a quart of small beer daily. Good cottages, with three bedrooms and exceptional conveniences, are let to 8 per cent. of the good working men at 3s. 6d. per week, rates and gas and water included. Tools and implements are supplied . Of maltsters, 25 per cent. have regular work, and 75 per cent. work on an average 32 weeks. Of storeroom men (preparers and deliverers) 20 per cent. have constant, whilst 80 per cent. have 32 weeks' employment. In the last 25 years maltsters' wages have risen 35 per cent. Storeroom labourers' wages have been advanced in the same time by about 28 per cent.

In brewing, able-bodied men earn 17s., a few 18s.; old men and youths have from 14s.; boys from 13s. to 7s. per week. No women or children are employed. Adult wages commence at seventeen years. Weekly average for six months, 59 contract men earned £1 8s. 2d. Thirty foremen, clerks, &c., £1 5s. 5d; 27 smellers, firing men, general stores, and stationery, £1 0s. 8d.; 21 coopers, £1 14s. 6d.; labourers, 90 men, 17s. 1d.; 60 boys, 8s. 11½d. They work nine and a half hours per day the first five days, 6½ hours on Saturday—54 hours per week. Each man receives one quart of ale per day, each boy one pint per day. At Christmas each married man receives 10lbs. beef; each single man, 6lbs.; boys, 4lbs. Foremen and outdoor clerks are supplied with overcoats and umbrellas; firemen with jackets, drawers, and clogs; drainers and stackers with jackets, and 7s. per year in lieu of clogs. A few cottages are let at a reduced rent. All tools are supplied.

Workmen are employed all the year. Contract men usually earn a little less three months in the summer.

In another brewery boys earn 8s. to 15s.; men, 18s. to 22s.; foremen, 24s. to 38s. All are paid by the week. No women. Adult wages commence at eighteen. Six per cent. on piecework, but only employed six months of the year. Average, £2 per week. Eleven per cent. are boys, 8 per cent. foremen, 81 per cent. men. The working hours are 59 in summer and 61 in winter. A daily allowance of ale is given. Maximum, 3 pints good ale, and 2 of small beer; minimum, 2 pints of ale. Boys get 1 to 2 pints, according as their age approaches eighteen. All tools are supplied. Sixty-five per cent. are employed all the year round, the remainder return to agricultural and other occupations for about six months. In the last fourteen years labourers' wages (the lowest class) have risen from 14s. to 18s. per week.

CORN MILLERS, BAKERS, AND CONFECTIONERS.

Sub-Order 3.

The wages of millers are given at 30s. per week, and the same for bakers, confectioners earning somewhat more. A journeyman baker receives besides his wages partial board and lodging. The work is arduous, and long hours are greatly complained of.

SUGAR REFINING.

Sub-Order 3.

In 1880 pan men earned in Bristol 45s. per week; Glasgow, 40s.; Greenock, 33s. to 40s., and London, 43s. Now they earn 40s. Sugar-house men in 1880 earned in Bristol, 19s.; in Glasgow, 22s.; in Greenock, 21s. 3d.; and in London, 30s., partly by time and partly by piecework. Present wages are given at 19s. 6d. Charcoal men in 1880 earned in Bristol, 19s. 6d.; Glasgow, 22s. 9d.; Greenock, 20s. to 25s.; London, 24s. Present wages, 19s. Stokers in 1880 earned in Bristol, 22s.; Glasgow, 25s.; Greenock, 23s.; London, 30s. Now they are stated to be earning 24s. In sugar refining the hours of labour are 61. In 100 men and boys employed, 52 are sugar-house men, 19 charcoal-house men, and 29 others.

H

CHOCOLATE MANUFACTURE.

Sub-Order 3.

Memorandum of Wages in a Chocolate and Cocoa Manufactory employing over 1000 hands in all departments.

MEN AND BOYS.

	Per Week of 56 hours.	
Young Men and Beginners	16/- to 20/-	Day Work.
More experienced Hands	20/- ,, 25/-	,, ,,
Superintendents, Timekeepers, &c.	up ,, 32/-	,, ,,
Lads and Young Men	10/- ,, 16/-	,, ,,
Younger Boys	4/- ,, 10/-	,, ,,
Men employed in Sugar Boiling and Confectionery Departments	30/- ,, 37/-	Piecework.
Younger Assistants in ditto	15/- ,, 18/-	,, ,,
Machine Box Makers	29/- ,, 31/6	,, ,,
Hand Box Makers	20/- ,, 30/-	,, ,,
Packers	28/- ,, 32/-	,, ,,

(General Factory Operatives)

Most of the above hands frequently work overtime, and consequently earn more than the rates specified above. There are also certain allowances, including a bonus of 6d. per week to men, and 3d. per week to boys, for punctual attendance, which are practically equivalent to an increase of wages of about 1s. per week to men, and 6d. per week to boys.

Fitters, carpenters, and other mechanics employed by the firm are paid at the current rates of wages in the district for their respective trades.

FEMALE DEPARTMENT.

	Age.	Per week of 50 hours.	Per week of 56 hours.
Cocoa Packers and Labellers	16 to 25	8/- to 11/-	12/- to 12/6
Young Girls with Packers	14	4/6 ,, 5/6	5/- ,, 6/6
Girls engaged in the Chocolate Cream Manufacturing, Packing Fancy Boxes, &c.	16 to 25	5/- ,, 10 -	10/- ,, 15/-

Other miscellaneous work at about the same rate.

Women and girls are mostly paid by piecework. When they are paid by time, the wages would generally be arranged according to the special circumstances of each case.

The above memorandum gives a fair average of the earnings in the different departments. In taking a lengthened period, some deduction must, of course, be made for loss of time through illness and other causes. This to some extent is compensated by sick pay during illness, provided for, in the case of the girls, by a charge of 1d. per week on all hands, and some other sources; and, in the case of the men, by the firm, where deemed needful.

The men, in many departments, earn a considerable addition to their wages by overtime, especially during the busy season. We have taken a few typical cases, and find that for the year ending 30th June last the overtime amounted to about 13 per cent. in addition to the standing wages. The females cannot, as a rule, owing to the operations of the Factory Act, earn what can strictly be called overtime, although we regard the standard hours of work for *them* as 50 per week, and treat any extra time in the nature of overtime. The memorandum will, however, explain this.

The workpeople are paid directly by the firm, as we do not encourage the system of workmen employing others under them. If they ever do so, it is in very exceptional cases.

The memorandum refers to some of the advantages enjoyed in addition to wages. Food is not provided, except that the men and boys have an allowance of tea and sugar. Material is also provided for some part of their working dress. The workpeople generally have the use of fires for cooking their food, and other accommodation during their meal times.

Except in the case of mechanics working at their own trades, the tools and implements are in almost every case supplied by the firm.

The works are carried on without interruption throughout the year, except during public holidays, and a day or two for summer outing. The piece-workers occasionally work short time, but this is probably more than made up by excess of work at other times.

We have not the means of readily giving accurately the fluctuations of wages during a period of years, but, speaking in general terms, the earnings are very considerably higher that they were 20 or 30 years ago.

Order XVII.

PERSONS WORKING IN THE TEXTILE FABRICS.

TEXTILE FABRICS.

The Factory Returns show that in 1878 there were 6449 factories for cotton, woollen, worsted, silk, flax, hemp, and jute, with an aggregate of 52,789,576 spindles, including 712,316 power looms, doubling and giving employment to 917,735 persons. In comparison with 1861 the factories are larger—16,532 spindles to one in 1878 against 10,525 to one in 1861; and whereas in 1861 there was one person employed to 67·29 spindles, in 1878 the proportion was one person to 91·54 spindles. A greater contrast, however, is shown by going into Mr. Porter's figures in his "Progress of the Nation" in 1839 in the Woollen and Cotton Industries, with those in the Factory Returns in 1878 :—

WOOLLEN FACTORIES.	1839.		1878.	
Ages.	Males.	Females.	Males.	Females.
Under 13 years	3,501	2,703	5,194	4,216
13 to 18 years	11,012	—	11,258	—
Over 13 years	—	18,817	—	65,848
18 years and upwards	18,746	—	47,828	—
	33,259	21,520	64,280	70,064

COTTON FACTORIES.	1839.		1878.	
Ages.	Males.	Females.	Males.	Females.
Under 13 years	7,106	5,211	28,663	33,260
13 to 18 years	41,287	—	34,730	—
Over 13 years	—	94,184	—	264,171
18 years and upwards	64,548	—	122,029	—
	112,941	146,355	185,472	297,431

Thus we find that whereas in 1839 there were employed 62 per cent. males and 38 per cent. females, in 1878 the proportion was 47 males and 53 females. There are more children employed now in the cotton manufacture —viz., 12·80 per cent. in 1878 against 4·73 in 1839 on the half-time system; and taken both together there were employed more men, 18 years and upwards, in 1878 than in 1839—viz., 27·52 per cent. in 1878 against 26·52 per cent. in 1839. The great extension of machinery has therefore not displaced but increased largely the work for human labour.

OF THE WORKING CLASSES.

WOOLLEN MANUFACTURE.

SUB-ORDER 1.

IN 1856, Mr. Edward Baines estimated the annual value of the Woollen Manufactures of the United Kingdom at £20,290,000. There were then used 76,000,000 lbs. of foreign and Colonial wool. In 1883 there were used 219,000,000 lbs. of foreign and Colonial wool. In 1856 there were 2030 Woollen and Worsted factories, with 3,111,521 spindles. In 1878 there were 2425 Woollen and Worsted factories, with 4,434,427 spindles. At the lowest calculation the present annual value of the Woollen Manufacture may be estimated at £36,000,000.

NUMBER OF WOOLLEN AND WORSTED FACTORIES.

Year.	No. of Factories.	No. of Spindles.	No. of Power Looms.	No. of Persons engaged.
1856	2030	3,111,521	53,409	166,885
1878	2425	6,208,695	144,337	265,269

QUANTITIES OF WOOL IMPORTED, EXPORTED, AND CONSUMED.

—	1840.	1860.	1880.	1883.
	lbs.	lbs.	lbs.	lbs.
Imported ..	49,436,284	148,396,577	463,508,963	495,946,779
Exported ..	1,014,625	30,761,867	237,408,589	277,234,084
Consumed ..	48,421,659	117,634,710	226,100,374	218,712,695

VALUE OF EXPORTS.

—	1840.	1860.	1880.	1883.
	£	£	£	£
Woollen and Worsted Yarn	452,957	3,843,450	3,344,740	3,266,488
Manufactured	5,327,853	12,156,998	17,265,177	18,315,576
Total ..	5,780,810	16,000,448	20,609,917	21,582,064

The wages in the Leeds woollen district, from 1795 to 1857 was given by Sir Edward Baines in a paper on the Woollen Manufacture of England, read before the British Association in 1858,* and with them we may compare the present wages as follows:—

Year.	Woollen Sorters.		Slubbers.		Spinners.		Dressers.			
	s.	d.	s.	d.	s.	d.	s.	d.	s.	d.
1795	—		22	6	16	9				
1805	31	1	30	8	24	8				
1815	37	8	30	6 (1816)	31	8				
1825	29	3	26	7 (1827)	20	4 (1826)	21	0 to	22	0
1835	26	9	24	9 (1833)	37	1†	20	0 ,,	21	0
1845	22	4	29	6 (1844)	34	11†	20	0 ,,	21	8
1855	20	8	24	0	29	0†	20	0 ,,	21	0
1867	22	0	—		—		18	0 ,,	22	0
1883	26	0	—		—		26	0 ,,	—	

SILK MANUFACTURE.

Sub-Order 2.

Number of Silk Factories.

Year.	No. of Factories.	No. of Spindles.	No. of Power Looms.	No. of Persons engaged.
1856	460	1,093,790	9,260	56,137
1878	706	1,018,939	12,540	40,985

Quantities Imported, Exported, and Consumed.

—	1840.	1860.	1880.	1883.
	lbs.	lbs.	lbs.	lbs.
Imported ..	3,759,016	9,178,647	8,673,949	3,178,593
Exported ..	147,059	3,153,993	947,165	524,182
Consumed ..	3,611,959	6,024,654	2,726,784	2,654,411

* Journal of the Statistical Society, Vol. 22, p. 1.

† Mules introduced, and workmen earned at half the price paid to the Jenny spinners—40s., less the 12s. to the piecers.

VALUE OF EXPORTS.

	1840.	1860.	1880.	1883.
	£	£	£	£
Silk, Thrown	37,528	826,107	683,591	705,825
Twist & Yarn	755,120	1,587,303	2,030,659	2,426,299
Total ..	792,648	2,413,410	2,714,250	3,132,124

The wages in the silk manufacture in Manchester in 1839, 1849, 1859 were given by Mr. Chadwick as follows:—

SILK THROWING AND MANUFACTURE.	1839. 66¼ hours per week.	1849. 60 hours per week.	1859. 60 hours per week.	1883. —
	s. d.	s. d.	s. d.	s. d. s. d.
Throwsters	13 0	13 0	17 0	17 0 to 20 0
Spinners (Young Men and Boys)	7 6	7 6	10 0	16 0 —
Winders (Women) ..	6 6	6 6	7 6	9 0 ,, 11 6
Cleaners (Girls & Young Women)	5 0	5 0	6 0	5 6 ,, 15 6

The silk manufacture is carried on partly in factories and partly in private houses, each weaver having one or more looms; Spitalfields and Macclesfield being the seats of silk and silk velvets, and Coventry of ribbons. The loom usually belongs to the weaver, and the cost is £2 to £4. Raw material of some value is entrusted with the labourer.

COTTON MANUFACTURE.

SUB-ORDER 3.

IN 1859 Mr. Chadwick estimated that 400,000 persons were engaged in the Cotton Manufacture, whose wages at 10s. 3¼d. per week would amount to £205,833 per week, or £10,653,000 per annum. In 1880-82 Mr. Ellison estimated that 686,000 operatives were engaged, and that at £42 per annum they would earn £28,812,000. In 1859 Mr. Chadwick estimated the capital invested in the Cotton Manufacture at £52,400,000. In 1876 Dr. Isaac Watt, in his articles on Cotton in the ninth edition of the "Encyclopædia Britannica," estimated the capital so invested at £90,000,000.

NUMBER OF COTTON FACTORIES.

Year.	No. of Factories.	No. of Spindles.	No. of Power Looms.	No. of Persons Employed.
1856	2210	28,010,217	298,847	379,213
1878	2674	44,206,190	514,911	482,903

QUANTITIES OF COTTON IMPORTED, EXPORTED, AND CONSUMED.

—	1840.	1860.	1880.	1883.
Imported ...	Cwt. 5,290,072	Cwt. 12,419,096	Cwt. 15,541,648	Cwt. 15,485,121
Exported ...	345,297	2,235,970	2,005,155	2,207,400
Consumed...	4,944,775	10,183,126	13,536,493	13,277,721

VALUE OF EXPORTS.

	1840.	1860.	1880.	1883.
Cotton Yarn Manufactured	£ 7,101,308 17,567,010	£ 9,870,875 42,141,505	£ 11,901,623 63,662,433	£ 13,509,732 62,936,025
Total...	24,668,318	52,012,380	75,564,056	76,445,757

The wages in the cotton manufacture have been given with much fulness by Mr. Lord, late President of the Manchester Chamber of Commerce, and I cannot do better than reproduce the tables given by him as follows:—

FINE SPINNING AND WEAVING.—BOLTON.

WAGES EARNED WEEKLY IN

Description.	Male or Female.	1850. s. d.	1860. s. d.	1870. s. d.	1877. s. d.	1883. s. d.	Average percentage Increase in each Trade between 1850 and 1883.
Strippers and Grinders..	M.	10 0	12s. & 13s.	17s. & 18s.	21 0	21 0	
Rovers ..	F.	6 8	8 0	16 0	17 0	16 0	
Minders..	M.	43 0	34 6	40 0	47 0	46 0	} 35·16
Winders..	F.	9 0	10 0	9 0	11 0	11 6	
Weavers ..	M. & F.	4 7 (per loom)	5 2	4 9	5 9	5 6	
Mechanics ..	M.	25 0	24s. to 26s.	28s. to 30s.	35s. to 38s.	35s. to 38s.	
Tacklers..	M.	29 0	32 0	37 0	30 3	35 6	
Percentage increase on 1850..		..	Unchanged.	15·13	37·72	35·16	35·16

NOTE.—Hours of Labour to 1874, 60 hours per week.
" " from 1874, 56½ " "

COTTON SPINNING—FINE.

Description.	Male or Female.	Wages Earned Weekly in 1850.		1860.		1870.		1877.		1883.		Average percentage increase in each Trade between 1850 and 1883.
		s.	d.	s.	d.	s.	d.	s.	d.	s.	d.	
Spinners—Hand-mules	M.	38	0	38	0	36	0	53	0	40	0	⎫
Cyphers	M.	11	0	11	0	15	0	16	6	16	0	⎬ 16·27
Piecers	F.	6	6	6	6	11	0	11	0	11	0	⎪
Creelers	F.	5	8	5	8	6	0	6	3	7	0	⎭
Mechanics	M.	30	0	30	0	32	0	32	0	32	0	
Percentage increase on 1850				Unchanged		9·68		30·21		16·27		
Drawing Tenters	F.	*No return.		*No return.		10	6	10	6	10	6	
Jack Tenters	F.	*No return.		*No return.		9	6	10	0	10	0	
Grinders	M.	*No return.		*No return.		21	6	23	6	23	6	
Minders—Self-actors	M.	*No return.		*No return.		35	0	38	0	38	0	

* For these years no returns have been made, but the difference is so slight that it would not affect the general average from which these items have been excluded.

NOTE.—Hours of Labour to 1874, 60 hours per week.
,, ,, from 1874, 56¼ ,, ,,

COTTON SPINNING AND WEAVING—MEDIUM QUALITY.

Description.	Male or Female.	Wages Earned Weekly in				Average percentage increase in each Trade between 1850 and 1883.
		1850.	1860.	1870.	1877.	1883.
		s. d.	s. d.	s. d.	s. d.	s. d.
Strippers and Grinders	M.	10 6	13 0	16 0	19 0	21 0	
Rovers	F.	7 6	11 0	14 0	17 0	18 0	
Throstle Spinners	F.	7 6	10 0	13 0	15 0	15 0	
Minders	M.	12 6	15 0	18s. to 22s.	25s. to 28s.	25s. to 28s.	
Winders	F.	7 0	8 0	11 0	16 0	17 6	
Weavers	M. & F.	14 0	14 6	17 0	18 0	19 6	
Mechanics	M.	23 6	25 0	27 0	28 0	32 0	
Overlookers and Tacklers	M.	22 0	25 0	30 0	31s. to 36s.	36s. to 38s.	
Stone Masons	M.	20 0	23 0	28 0	30 0	30 0	
Labourers	M.	12 0	15 0	20 0	22 0	22 0	
Percentage increase on 1850		..	16·85	43·59	64·47	74·72	74·72

NOTE.—Hours of Labour to 1874, 60 hours per week.
,, ,, from 1874, 56½ ,, ,,

A VERY LARGE COTTON MILL, SPINNING No. 150 WEFT.

Description.	Male or Female.	Wages Earned Weekly in				Increase per cent.
		1850. Per 60 hours.	1860.	1870.	1877.	1883. Per 56 hours.	
		s. d.				s. d.	
Labourers	...	15 0	...	...	...	20 0	
Mechanics	...	27 0	...	...	...	33 0	
Strippers and Grinders	...	13 6	...	...	...	21 0	
Cardroom Overlookers	...	27 0	No returns.	No returns.	No returns.	32 0	
Roving Frame Tenters	...	8 3				14 0	
Drawing Tenters	...	8 3				11 0	
Combing Tenters (1853)	...	8 6				15 6	
Jack Tenters	...	8 0				16 6	
Spinners (hand)	...	40 0				52 0	
Big Piecers	...	13 0				16 0	
Spinners (self-actors)	...	...				42 0	
		168 6				231 0	37 %

NOTE.—Hours of Labour to 1874, 60 hours per week.
,,   ,,   ,,   from 1874, 56¼ ,,   ,,

FINE SPINNING.—BOLTON.

Description.	Male or Female.	Wages Earned Weekly in		
		1864.	1874.	1883.
		s. d.	s. d.	s. d.
Strippers and Grinders ..	M.	15 0	21 0	21 0
Jack Tenters	F.	12 0	15 0	15 11
Drawing Tenters ..	F.	8 6	11 6	14 9
Self-actor Minders ..	M.	28 2½	30 7	32 2
Piecers—big	M.	13 0	13 0	13 0
„ little	M.	6 0	8 6	8 9
Average increase in 1883 on 1864				31·26%

NOTE.—As this return is not for the same years as the others, it is not included in the General Summary.

NOTE.—Hours of Labour to 1874, 60 hours per week.
„ „ from 1874, 56½ „ „

BLEACHING.

Description.	Male or Female.	Wages Earned Weekly in					Average percentage increase in each Trade between 1850 and 1883.
		1850.	1860.	1870.	1877.	1883.	
		s. d.	s. d.	s. d.	s. d.	s. d.	
Dressers or Singers	M.	31 6	37 3	42 11	37 2	39 1	
Hand Crofters	,,	27 5	28 9	31 9	29 8	32 1	
Bleaching Machine—Foremen	,,	21 9	27 8	22 1	34 6	34 0	
,, ,, Minders	F. say	7 0	7 10	12 0	13 0	9 3	
,, ,, Pumpers	,, ,,	6 0	6 8	8 6	8 5	6 10	
,, ,, Plaiters	,, ,,	5 2	5 8	6 10	7 2	5 11	50%
Stiffeners	M.	29 8	39 7	51 4	69 10	75 9	
Assistant Stiffeners	,,	23 0	33 9	22 0	32 2	25 0	
Manglers	,,	21 11	30 8	25 1	34 1	28 8	
Calenderers	,,	22 2	38 2	36 3	39 10	30 9	
Driers	,,	19 8	26 7	24 0	34 8	27 9	
Makers-up	,,	18 5	26 9	21 10	26 10	32 8	
Hookers (age 16)	M. & F.	5 7	6 5	7 0	9 2	12 3	
Packers	M.	19 7	26 1	28 4	28 11	28 3	
Percentage increase on 1850	..	..	32·06	31·40	56·60	50·00	

Description.	Male or Female.	Percentage Advance on 1850.				Average percentage Increase in each Trade between 1850 and 1883.
		1850.	1860.	1870.	1877.	1883.	
Machine Printers	M.	...	8%	25%	50%	50%	50 %

The President of the Manchester Chamber of Commerce (Mr. G. Lord), in response to the desire expressed by the delegates of the Weaving Branch, at their meeting at Ashton-under-Lyne, published the following as the data on which he based his statement to the Chamber on Thursday last. The figures show the wages earned per week of 60 hours up to 1874, and of 56¼ hours since :—

Mill A.

	1850.	1860.	1870.	1877.	1883.	Increase, Weavers alone in 1883 on 1850.	Increase, Weavers and Winders together.
	s. d.	s. d.	s. d.	s. d.	s. d.		
Weavers....	9 6¼	15 1	13 10	18 6	16 0	67¼ per cent.	87¼ per cent.
Winders....	8 3	10 9	11 0	17 0	12 0	45¼ per cent.	

This is a large mill, and the weavers' earnings per week are arrived at by taking the total earnings of the shed and dividing that sum by the number of weavers employed. The reduction in earnings of weavers in 1870 was due to the fact that the material used at that time was not so good as that in use immediately before and since.

Mill B.

	1850.	1860.	1870.	1877.	1883.	Increase, Weavers in 1883 on 1850.	Increase, Weavers and Winders together.
	s. d.	s. d.	s. d.	s. d.	s. d.		
Weavers....	8 2	14 9	15 6	16 0	15 0	83½ per cent.	65 per cent.
Winders....	8 6	9 0	11 6	14 0	13 6	47 per cent.	

Mill C.

In 1850 a weaver received 10s. 4d. per week for attending to one pair of looms, now she receives 23s. for two pairs of looms, out of which she pays a tenter 5s. 3d., leaving her 17s. 9d. Taking weavers and winders together, the increase shown at this mill is 56¼ per cent.

Mill D.

In 1850 a weaver received 8s. for attending to one pair of looms, now she receives 24s. for attending to two pairs, and pays 6s. to a tenter, leaving her 18s. Taking weavers and winders together, the increase shown at this mill is 64¾ per cent.

Mill E.

In 1850 a weaver earned 9s. 2¼d., in 1883 earned 15s. 0½d. Increase, 63½ per cent.

Mr. Lord states that he has a number of other returns corroborative of those above given, but he thinks it "unnecessary to multiply proofs of facts so universally known to all in the trade."

A Cotton Manufacturer supplied the following particulars:—

Proportion of Persons employed per 100 hands.

1. In Spinning Department exactly List prices.
 In Weaving Department 10 per cent. under List prices.
2. Men employed in Card-room, 20s. per week ... 3·00
 Boys   „   „   13s. 10d. per week ... 2·50
 Children, 10 to 14 years of age, 2s. 6d. to 3s. for 28 hours ... ... 3·00
 Women. None by time.
 Adult wages begin when about 20.
3. Mule spinners, men, £2 5s. 6d., less 15s. per week... 8·50
 Card-room hands, women, 18s. per week ... ... 9·50
 Weavers (power loom), Weaving Cotton Goods—
 2-Loom Weavers, 11s. per week, boys and girls, 13 to 15 years of age ... ... 2·80
 3-Loom Weavers, 16s. 6d. per week, 12 per cent. men, 21 per cent. women ... ... 13·35
 4-Loom Weavers, 22s. per week, 27 per cent. men, 40 per cent. women ... ... 27·12
 Cop Winders, women, 15s. per week ... ... 6·73
 Warpers, women, 20s. per week ... ... 1·70
 Average earnings for 12 months taken from the Wage Book.
4. Foremen, 35s. per week ⎫   ⎧ 5·00
 Artisans, 33s. per week ⎬ No overt'me ...⎨ 3·00
 Labourers, 17s. 9d. per week ⎭   ⎩ 5·80
5. Mule spinners pay their piecers or assistants 15s. per week ... ... 8·50
6. Monday, Tuesday, Wednesday, Thursday, and Friday 10 hours per day, Saturday 6½ hours, making a total of 56½ per week.
7. None.
8. All tools or implements supplied.

9. Fifty-two weeks per year, holidays excepted, which amount to about one week per year.
10.   Spinning Department—
June 20, 1878, wages paid 10 per cent. under List.
April 2, 1879, advanced 5 per cent., making them 5 per cent. under List.
April 7, 1880, advanced 5 per cent., making them full List.

Weaving Department—
June 20, 1878, wages paid 10 per cent. under List.
April 2, 1879, wages reduced 5 per cent., making them 15 per cent. under List.
January 7, 1885, wages advanced 5 per cent., making them 10 per cent. under List.
February 14, 1884, wages reduced 5 per cent., making them 15 per cent. under List.
July 11, 1883, wages advanced 5 per cent., making them 10 per cent. under List.

100·00

LINEN MANUFACTURE.

Sub-Order 3.

Number of Flax Factories.

	No. of Factories.	No. of Spindles.	No. of Power Looms.	No. of Persons engaged.
1861	417	1,288,043	7,689	80,262
1878	400	1,329,248	40,448	108,806

Quantities Imported, Exported, and Consumed.

	1850.	1860.	1880.	1883.
	Cwt.	Cwt.	Cwt.	Cwt.
Imported	1,253,240	1,481,234	2,096,096	1,657,416
Exported	2,228	19,707	58,923	62,204
Consumed	1,251,012	1,461,527	1,947,173	1,595,212

VALUE OF EXPORTS.

	1840.	1860.	1880.	1883.
Linen Yarn	£ 822,816	£ 1,801,272	£ 1,211,542	£ 1,326,787
Manufactured	3,306,088	4,804,803	5,836,019	5,439,569
Total	4,128,964	6,606,075	7,047,561	6,766,356

In 1860 the wages in Leeds and neighbourhood for flax and tow were:—Spinners and overlookers, 22s.; mechanics and warehousemen, 18s.; spinners and twisters, females, 6s.; yarn and thread reelers, females, 7s.; preparers, boys, 4s. 10d.; weavers, females, 9s.; winders' warpers, females, 8s. per week. In 1880 the wages in Dundee were—Roughers, shacklers, 21s. to 25s.; sorters, lads and boys, 10s.; machine lads and boys, 7s. 3d.; tow carders, lads and boys, 7s. 6d.; women, 9s. 3d.; reelers' women, 10s. to 13s. 6d.; weaving tenters, 30s.; dressers, 25s.; weavers' women, 14s. In 1883 the wages were—sorters, 20s. to 26s.; weavers, 30s.; tenters, 32s. In Belfast the average wages of girls are 10s.; piecework tenters to attend the girls about 35s.; bleach work and dye work, 18s.

The wages in the jute manufacture are as follows:— Preparing foremen, men, 28s.; batchers' machine, women, 12s.; spinners, 11s. to 13s.; shifters, girls, 8s. 6d.; power loom weavers, 22s. to 27s. 6d.; women, 13s. 6d. to 15s. 6d.

ROPE MAKERS.

SUB-ORDER 4.

IN 1880 the wages in Dundee and neighbourhood were— Hemp dresses, 20s.; rope yarn spinners, 22s.; twine spinners, 22s.; lads and boys, 7s. 6d.; labourers, 18s.; rope makers, 22s.; sail maker, 25s. Present wages are—rope yarn, 22s. 6d.; hemp drawers, 24s.

Order XVIII.
PERSONS WORKING IN DRESS.

BOOT AND SHOE MAKERS.
Sub-Order 1.

THE Miscellaneous Statistics gave the wages at Leicester in 1880 at — Clickers (cutters out) men, 27s.; lads and boys, 8s. 6d.; sewing machinists, men, 30s.; women, 15s.; girls, 5s.; rough stuff cutters, men, 21s.; lads and boys, 8s.; riveters, men, piecework, 25s.; lads and boys, 7s. to 14s.; machine operators, men, 28s.; lads and boys, 7s. to 15s.; finishers, men, 30s.; lads and boys, 12s. to 15s., piecework. When the men work at their own homes the temptations to idle their time are greater than in a factory. It is not unusual for such men to take work from more than one employer.

HAT MANUFACTURE.
Sub-Order 1.

THE Miscellaneous Statistics gave the wages of Hat making at Manchester in 1880 at—Body makers, 24s. 6d. and 27s. 3d., piecework; women, 12s.; lads and boys, 8s. 9d.; proofers, men, 21s. 3d.; lads and boys, 11s.; blockers, men, 30s. 3d., piecework; day wages, 21s. 9d.; dyers, men, 20s. 6d.; lads and boys, 11s.; finishers, men, 26s.; trimmers, women, 13s.; girls, 7s. 9d., piecework; lashers, girls, 3s. 6d.; shapers, men, 23s. 3d., or piecework, 24s.

TAILORS AND SHIRT MAKERS.
Sub-Order 1.

THE wages of tailors differ materially in different parts of the country, and they range from 3d. to 5d. per hour, or 15s. to 38s. per week. The wages of shirt makers and dress makers are stated to average 15s. 3d., but they fluctuate from time to time, and from shop to shop at the same time. A large house reports that they pay the managers of their dressmaking department about £150 per annum with board and lodging, and that the manager has several first· hands under her, who cut and fit ladies dresses on and do a little sewing, whose wages are from £40 to £70 per annum, with board and lodging. Each first hand has the management of a room with, say, about 20 seamstresses, women and girls. The women get 16s. to 18s. per week; and the girls, 14 to 16 years old, get 10s. to 12s. These are all what are called day-workers, and live out of the house, having only their tea and bread and butter allowed at 4 p.m. Hours of labour, 8.30 a.m. to 7.30 p.m., half-hour allowed for each meal. A machinist gets 18s. per week, with tea, &c., same as other day-workers. There is a great deal of work done for shops by people who employ from 10 to 20 seamstresses, and this is nearly all piece-work. Shops give out a quantity of shirts and dresses, &c., to be made all alike, and bargain for them to be completed for a fixed sum, which is all done piece-work, and the seamstresses, if they apply themselves and work hard, often earn 20s. a week and more. Good workpeople can always get plenty of work and earn good wages, and if intelligent and painstaking soon get to be first or second hands. There are many private dressmakers in the West-End who employ from 5 to 20 or 30 women and girls, and many of whom live and board in the house with their mistresses, and get from £15 to £20 per year wages. There are also several factories in the City where there are some 200 or 300 people employed and take up for the wholesale; but they all earn good wages if they work hard and apply themselves, nearly as much as in the West-End, and this is all piece-work. The same with mantle makers.

GLOVE MANUFACTURE.

Sub-Order 1.

This is principally a domestic industry. Men can cut 14 to 25 dozen per week, and they may earn on an average 26s. The general average, however, is 16s. to 20s. A woman can make when she employs all her time in it 1½ dozen or 2 dozen per week; but few persons work at it all day, having household duties to attend to. The average wages are 5s. to 7s. per week; but a good hand will earn double that of a common hand. The sewing is almost invariably done separately from the embroidery, welting, &c., and by different hands. A good sewer can make 30 or 36 pair per week, and get 3s. 3d. per dozen pairs. A pointer, embroiderer, or welter can earn, according to her opportunities and capabilities, from 4s. to 5s. to 18s. or even 20s. per week.

Order XIX.
Persons working in animal substances.

SOAP AND CANDLE MANUFACTURE.

Sub-Order 1.

In Soap making, soap boilers in 1880 earned 37s. 6d. in Bristol and Liverpool, and 45s. to 60s. in London; soap house labourers—Bristol, 21s., Liverpool, 20s., London, 22s.; soda makers—Bristol, 28s. 3d. piece-work, Liverpool, 22s. 6d., London, 24s. to 30s.; soap cutters—Bristol and Liverpool, 21s. 6d., London, 22s. 6d.; labourers—Bristol, 19s., Liverpool, 21s., London, 22s.

In Candle making moulders earned—Bristol, 26s. 9d. piece-work, Liverpool, 25s., London, 28s.; packers—Bristol, 18s. 9d., Liverpool, 23s. 6d., London, 24s. to 30s.; foremen—Bristol, 45s. 6d., Liverpool, 30s. per week.

SKINNERS, TANNERS, AND CURRIERS.

Sub-Order 2.

In Tan-yards the wages are 20s. to 30s. per week, the proportion being one-third, 25s. to 30s., and two-thirds, 20s. to 25s., partly piecework, and partly by time. Fleshers earn 29s., shedmen, 28s. The labourers work 56 hours per week, and mostly all the year without interruption. They are allowed the ox-tails, and some with meat. All tools and implements are supplied to them. Saddlers in Manchester earn 28s., labourers, 20s.; slaughter-house men, Manchester, 24s. per week.

LEATHER CASE, AND OTHER WORKERS IN LEATHER.

Sub-Order 2.

In the finer work of leather, including leather case, portfolio, parchment, and vellum manufacture, the wages are higher than those of tanners and curriers. They range from 30s. to 35s. per week.

BRUSH MAKERS.

Sub-Order 3.

In the manufacture of hair, including the making of brushes and brooms, the wages in Manchester are 26s. men, 6s. to 8s. boys.

TANNERS.
SUB-ORDER 2.

PRESENT wages are given as follows:—Unhairers, 27s.; fleshers, 29s. 4d.; tanyard labourers, 23s. 7d.; shedmen, 28s. 4d.; labourers, 18s.

ORDER XX.
PERSONS WORKING IN VEGETABLE SUBSTANCES.

GUM, OIL, AND COLOURMEN.
SUB-ORDER 1.

THE wages in this industry are 25s. per week for men. In Hull, the wages of seed crushers were in 1880—Foremen, 35s. to 60s.; pressmen, 27s.; parers, 18s. 3d.; grinders, 21s.; oil house men, 24s.; cake stowers, 20s.; binmen, 18s. to 24s.; hair repairers, 24s.; engine drivers, 25s.; labourers, 20s.; lads and boys, 12s.

SAWYERS, COOPERS, AND TURNERS.
SUB-ORDER 3.

THE wages of sawyers in Manchester are 24s., sawmill labourers, 20s.; coopers in the dockyard earn 3s. 6d. to 4s. 6d. per day.

PAPER MANUFACTURE.
SUB-ORDER 4.

THE Paper Manufacture is scattered all over the country, but the great centres are on the banks of the Thames and in the vicinities of Edinburgh. In 1870 there were in all 344 paper mills with moving horse-power of 26,948 steam and 8312 water. But there were also factories for paper staining, cardboard making, envelope making, paper box making, &c.

In 1880 the wages in Edinburgh were—Papers makers, 20s.; glazers and sorters, women, 10s.; finishers, women, 12s.; rag sorters and cutters, women, 10s. 6d.; stokers, men, 24s.; mechanics, 26s.; labourers, 15s.; Esparto workers, 13s. to 20s.; women, 10s. In London, paper makers earned 30s.; assistant lads, 14s. ; finishers, men, 25s. ; lads and boys, 9s. ; rag sorters and cutters, women, 10s. 6d. ; stokers, 25s. ; labourers, 21s. Present wages in Edinburgh are given as follows :—Paper makers, 21s. ; glazers, 20s. ; stokers, 23s. to 25s. ; labourers, 16s. to 19s. 6d. ; paperhangers' designers, 50s. ; packers, 22s. 2d.

Order XXI.

PERSONS WORKING IN MINERAL SUBSTANCES.

Some idea of the wealth which lies under our feet in these fortunate isles may be formed from the following quantities and value of Minerals produced in 1883 :—

Description.	Quantity.	Value at the Mine.
	Statute Tons.	£
Coal	163,737,327	46,054,143
Iron Ore	17,383,046	5,122,381
Clay	2,853,353	706,757
Slates and Slabs	498,062	1,246,332
Lead Ore	53,980	436,500
Tin Ore	14,469	735,189
Copper Ore	46,288	145,904
Others	—	1,351,675
		55,798,881

The production of Coal and Iron has considerably increased within recent years, as will be seen from the following. The number employed in coal mines has more than doubled since 1855 :—

Year.	Coal.	Pig Iron.	No. of Persons employed in Coal Mines.
	Tons.	Tons.	
1855	61,453,079	3,218,154	242,719
1860	80,042,698	3,826,752	275,847
1865	98,150,587	4,819,254	315,451
1870	110,431,192	5,963,515	350,894
1875	131,867,105	6,365,105	535,845
1880	146,818,622	7,749,233	484,933
1883	156,499,977	8,586,080	514,933

COAL MINING.

Sub-Order 1.

THE earnings of colliers were given in Symon's "Arts and Artizans," as contributed by William Dixon, Esq., the largest proprietor of collieries, as follows :—

Year.	Average earnings per day.	Average earnings per week, assuming 4½ days of 10 hours as the average quantity of work wrought by each collier per week, with house free and coal free, except his own labour in producing.	Total earnings per week, including house rent, which is given gratis, and coals.
	s. d.	£ s. d.	£ s. d.
1811	4 11	1 2 1½	1 4 8½
1815	4 6	1 0 3	1 2 5
1820	3 9	0 16 10½	0 18 9½
1825	5 3	1 3 7½	1 6 5½
1830	4 3	0 19 1½	1 0 11½
1835	4 0	0 18 0	0 19 9

Present wages in Durham were given in July, 1884, as follows : — Colliers, from 3s. 9d., 4s. to 4s. 9d. per day. The difference arises from the many kinds of engines to be worked, and from the difference of the men's ability. Those receiving 4s. work 8 hours per day, they being the most numerous and also the most important — viz., winding the coal out of the mines, raising and lowering the miners up and down to their work. This class comprises one half of the whole of the enginemen employed in and about the mines. Those receiving 3s. 9d. and 4s. 9d., the former work above ground, the latter below ground, each work from 10½ to 12 hours per day. Their numbers being equal a quarter each of the whole, as above referred to.

It is gratifying to find that the danger of accidents in coal mining has greatly diminished in recent years. In the five years from 1855 to 1859 there was one death from accidents for every 260 persons employed. In the four years from 1880 to 1883 there was one death for every 473 persons employed.

The wages in Mr. Lord's tables in Manchester were given as follows :—

COAL MINING.

Description.	Male or Female.	Wages Earned Weekly in				Average percentage increase in each Trade between 1850 and 1883.
		1850.	1860.	1870.	1877.	1883.	
		s. d.	s. d.	s. d.	s. d.	s. d.	
Colliers	M.	19 6	25 8	24 5	28 7	26 3	
Engineers	,,	18 5	22 0	23 9	35 8	32 6	
Smiths	,,	23 6	24 3	27 7	31 1	29 4	43·53
Joiners	,,	21 3	22 10	24 6	34 9	30 5	
Carters	,,	15 4	16 8	17 1	21 9	18 2	
Draymen	,,	14 3	16 5	18 6	23 11	21 2	
Dischargers	,,	16 4	17 2	15 9	18 10	20 2	
Bricklayers	,,	18 10	36 0	32 2	34 10	33 7	
Percentage increase on 1850	..	..	22·78	24·64	55·64	43·53	

GAS WORKS.
SUB-ORDER 2.

IN the manufacture of gas in Birmingham 20·73 per cent. are ordinary stokers, 28·23 per cent. labourers, 5·08 per cent. retort labourers, 6·52 per cent. coal porters, 9·65 per cent. coke fillers, and the remaining 29·79 per cent. bricklayers, pipe layers, meter makers, &c., only 9·24 per cent. consisting of gas makers, leading stokers.

The wages in 1880 were higher than at present. They are now given as follows:—

Gas Makers	38s. 2d.
Stokers	36s. 6d.
Retort Labourers	19s. 2d.
Coal Porters	29s. 0d.
Coke Fillers	29s. 0d.
Engine Drivers	32s. 6d.
Carpenters	37s. 6d.
Bricklayers	38s. 7d.
Smiths	36s. 0d.
Strikers	17s. to 25s. 6d.
Gas Fitters	33s. 6d.
Outside Fitters	30s. 9d.
Pipe Layers	30s. 0d.
Lamplighters	22s. 4d.
Plumbers	26s. 2d.
Glazers	26s. 10d.
Labourers	24s. 10d.

QUARRYMEN.
SUB-ORDER 3.

THE wages of quarrymen are 30s.; boring, 21s.; stone dressers, 32s.; stone cutters, 21s. In Manchester the wages of paviours are given as 26s., and labourers 20s.; bricksetters, 36s.

BRICKMAKING.
SUB-ORDER 3.

THE wages in the Brick and Tile Manufacture are given as follows:—Millmen, 19s.; brickmakers, 21s. to 26s.; pipemakers, 19s. to 21s.; retort makers, 29s.; labourers, 17s.

EARTHENWARE AND GLASS.
SUB-ORDER 4.

IN the Earthenware Manufacture in 1870 there were 498 factories employing moving power to the extent of 2858 horse-power steam, and 48 horse-power water. The Potteries had 541 factories, with 5261 horse-power steam, and 360 horse-power water.

The wages have been as follows:—

	1858-60.	1880.	1884.
	Per day.	Per week.	
Claymakers	4s.	30s. to 35s.	45s. 6d. per week
Throwers	7s.	40s. to 48s.	7s. per day
Turners	6s. 6d.	25s. to 38s.	53s. 6d. per week
Handlers	5s.	32s. to 36s.	5s. per day
Pressers—Hollow wares	5s.	30s. to 35s.	5s. ,,
Flat ,,	6s.	35s.	3s. ,,
Moulders	5s.	33s. to 40s.	6s. 6d. ,,
Saggar Makers	5s.	25s. to 30s.	
Biscuit Firemen	6s.	45s. to 60s.	7s. ,,
Placers	4s. 6d.	30s.	
Gilders	6s.	25s.	5s. ,,
Enamellers, Women	1s. 9d.	10s. 6d.	
Gloat Firemen	6s.	60s.	
Placers	4s. 6d.	30s. to 35s.	5s. ,,

The exports of earthenware, porcelain, and glass of the United Kingdom have progressed as follows:—

Year.	Earthenware and Porcelain.	Glass.
	£	£
1840	573,184	417,178
1850	998,448	307,755
1860	1,450,644	653,198
1870	2,746,153	832,716
1880	2,065,518	921,608
1883	2,333,167	1,084,434

In London in the Art Department of an important earthenware manufacture, the present rate of wage varies from 3s. 6d. per week up to £4 or £5. The average rate paid to men is 38s.; women, 28s.; children, 9s. 6d.; adult wages begin at 21 years. The average piece-work earnings are—Artists, 30s.; assistants, 14s. The proportion of assistants to artists in amount of wages is about twice of assistants to that of artists. All wages are paid direct, and have no reductions except 4d. per week for savings fund, and 4d. per week for sick fund, both of which are compulsory. The time of work is 5 days of 7 hours and 1 day of 4½ hours. Dining and tea accommodation is provided free, and provisions at nominal charges. Tools and implements are supplied to day-workers, but not to piece-workers. Fifty weeks may be counted for the annual earning. There is no fluctuation of wage.

The wages in the Glass manufacture are as follows:— Blowers, 40s.; pressed-glass men, 30s.; apprentices, 10s.; glass cutters, 30s.; pot makers, 30s.; founders, 28s.; packers, 30s.

GOLDSMITHS, SILVERSMITHS, JEWELLERS.

Sub-Order 7.

The factory returns of 1870 gave 43 factories in England for gold and silver plate and jewellery, and 99 for electro-plate ware.

In 1880 the wages in electro-plated wares were given in Birmingham as follows:—Brazier men, 36s. to 58s.: brushmen, 26s. to 33s.; stampers, 29s. to 38s.; buffers, 26s. to 34s.; polishers and finishers, 29s. to 38s.; lathmen, 29s. to 38s.; chasers and engravers, 35s. to 58s.; castors, 39s. to 58s.; spinners, 39s. to 58s.; burnishers (women), 13s. to 19s.; makers-up, 36s. to 44s.

The following interesting remarks on the earnings of goldsmiths in London have been kindly supplied by a leading firm:—

There are two causes which would mainly remove the statistics regarding them from those which would affect the labouring classes of this country generally. Their wages must necessarily be higher, because of the great intrinsic value of the material employed, which renders it necessary to raise them above temptation, and the artistic character of the work ranks them amongst those who are on the borderland of the artist and the sculptor.

Our trade may be divided into four departments—work in silver, work in gold, the setting of stones, and the cutting of rough stones or the recutting of those which arrive from the East in an imperfect form. At our silver manufactory in Harrison-street the workmen are divided into four classes— —casters, silversmiths, chasers, and polishers. They work 58 hours in each week. The first-named earn from 30s. to 50s. per week; the second, from 35s. to 55s.; the third, from 35s. to 60s.; the polishers, from 25s. to 36s. The lowest wage begins, after the seven years' apprenticeship ends, at 21 years, but there is a small payment before this, according to the usefulness of the man. We supply all tools except to the chasers. The men have one day and a half in the year without work of which they receive pay.

This rate of wages has remained stationary during all the time of our experience. If the demand for good artistic handwork in silver had increased in proportion to the increase of wealth and population, it is highly probable that the rate of wages would have advanced also, but the introduction of electro-plating gave a blow to the manufacture of silver from which it has never recovered.

Apprenticeship has, we may say, gone out of fashion in our trade. We believe that the reason for this is to be found in the fact that dishonesty being suspected and not proved, it was considered more convenient to have the power to discharge an apprentice rather than to be under the necessity of proving a charge or to keep him still in the workshop. We use the word apprenticeship, therefore, as meaning a term of instruction, and not the binding agreement of former days still existing in most trades.

Our workmen are not paid by piece-work, but we believe that it is very general in our trade to do so. As a rule, higher wages can be obtained in this way for short periods, but the firms which adopt these principles are not generally in a position to give permanent occupation to men, and, therefore, it is precarious.

Workmen in gold are paid from 1s. to 1s. 9d. an hour, and work 50 hours in the week. Boys are not apprenticed, but are paid 5s. a week at first, and by end of their term of instruction can earn about 20s. per week. All tools are found for the men.

Diamond setters are paid from 36s. to 80s. per week of 50 hours, but in our own place they have extra privileges, which reduce the time to 47 hours. The term of apprenticeship is seven years, but there are no indentures.

We also employ women to polish the settings, as their touch is lighter than that of men. After an apprenticeship of three years they can earn from 24s. to 30s. per week of 47 hours.

There are very few lapidaries, and it is most difficult to find good workmen in this branch of our trade, which, nevertheless, presents a wide field of usefulness and advantage. The wages range from 30s. to 60s. per week of about 50 hours, but an intelligent man who learns to treat a valuable stone with judgment can, of course, earn far more than this.

The art of diamond cutting is a branch of that of the lapidary, and there is no reason why it should not be developed in this country, and give profitable employment to a large number of people.

IRON MANUFACTURE.

Sub-Order 8.

The Iron Industry includes blast furnaces, iron mills, foundries, machinery, hardware and other minor industries, and in 1870 there were 4267 factories for the same, with an aggregate of 289,352 horse steam power and 6043 horse water power. The exports have increased rapidly as follows :—

Year.	Iron and Steel.		Machinery.	Implements.	Hardware and Cutlery.
	Tons.	£	£	£	£
1840	268,000	2,524,000	593,000	..	1,319,000
1850	783,000	5,350,000	1,042,000	..	2,641,000
1860	1,442,000	12,154,000	3,838,000	..	3,771,000
1870	2,826,000	24,038,000	5,293,000	326,000	3,812,000
1880	3,793,000	28,391,000	9,263,000	378,000	3,521,000
1883	4,043,000	28,590,000	13,433,000	853,000	3,756,000

And, according to Mr. Lord's table, the wages have progressed as follows :—

OF THE WORKING CLASSES. 143

Description.	Male or Female.	Wages Earned Weekly in				Average percentage Increase in each Trade between 1850 and 1883.
		1850.	1860.	1870.	1877.	1883.
		s. d.	s. d.	s. d.	s. d.	s. d.
Puddlers	M.	45 0	40 0	40 0	45 0	46 0	Decrease 14·88
Hammermen	,,	70 0	60 0	60 0	65 0	65 0	
Forge Rollers	,,	50 0	45 0	45 0	50 0	50 0	
Ball Furnacemen or Heaters ..	,,	60 0	50 0	60 0	65 0	50 0	
Wire Rollers	,,	120 0	130 0	100 0	120 0	120 0	
,, Drawers	,, say	80 0	80 0	80 0	56 0	45 0	
Galvanizers	,,	80 0	50 0	50 0	43 0	40 0	
Mechanics	,,	28 0	30 0	30 0	31 0	31 0	
Labourers	,,	18 0	18 0	20 0	20 0	20 0	
Percentage decrease on 1850..	..	..	8·78	11·98	10·16	14·88

Present wages in the iron manufacture are given as follows: —Moulders, 32s. 3d.; pattern makers, 32s.; turner planes, 29s.; drillers, 19s.; boilers, 29s.; holders up, 24s.; smiths, 33s. 6d.; labourers, 19s. 6d. And in the iron and steel manufacture—Smelters, 38s. 6d.; moulders, 35s. 9d.; gas producers, 28s. 9d.; fitters, 29s.; turners, 28s. 6d.; bar rollers, 18c, 30s.; 14c, 27s.

The mode of working, and condition of employment, and wages were described as follows by a leading manufacturer in Birmingham on the 28th December, 1878 :—

In South Staffordshire it is usual for puddlers to commence work about 4 o'clock on Monday afternoon, continuing night and day with double sets of workmen until about 1 to 3 o'clock on Saturday.

This arrangement provides five turns' (*days*) work for each set per week, the number of working hours per turn (day) depends upon the quality and character of the pig iron—viz., rich, poor, grey, mottle, or white, also to the number of furnaces working to one hammer.

The old puddling furnace is built for charges of 4 cwt. of pig iron. We charge 4½ cwt. to 5 cwt. per heat, and the men work 6 heats per day. This usually occupies from 10 to 11 hours. Each puddler employs an underhand to assist in firing, cleaning, and fettling the furnace; also in melting, boiling, drawing the heats, and charging the furnace, the underhand being in constant attendance, and usually doing most of the work. The puddler helps to charge the furnace, finishes the boiling until crude iron is formed. He then separates the particles, and balls the iron into a convenient shape, and when ready, takes or sends the balls to the hammer. The actual time that the puddler is before the heat of the furnace does not average more than 5 hours per day, or 25 hours per week. It is, however, fair to say that the steady, attentive workman is usually found at his furnace doing something to forward the process. In addition to the pig-iron it is also customary to supply to each furnace during every 12 hours sufficient scrap iron to make two balls about 120 lbs. each. The rate paid for puddling is 7s. 6d. per ton (of 2400 lbs.), and for balling scraps 6s. 6d. per ton (of 2400 lbs.). In works where the charge is only 4 cwt. the average daily earnings of the puddler will be about 6s. to 6s. 6d. per day, or 30s. to 35s. per week, and that of the underhand 16s. to 18s. per week.

The extra charge in our case—and this is by no means exceptional—enables our puddlers to earn from 34s. to 38s., and in some cases 40s. per week, and that of the underhand from 17s. to 20s. per week.

The shinglers receive the puddle balls at the hammer from the puddler, working the iron into blooms, or into a suitable shape for the rolls. For this they are paid at the rate of about 1s. 2d. to 1s. 6d. per ton (of 2400 lbs.).

We pay one rate of 1s. 3d. per ton. This is the lowest rate paid by the writer during the past 20 years. Each shingler employs assistants, and pays day wages. The average income of foreman is regulated by the number of furnaces in operation, and varies from 8s. to 14s. per day, or 40s. to 70s. per week.

The following will fairly represent the average earnings of this class of workmen:—Foremen shinglers, 8s. to 14s. per day, or 40s. to 70s. per week; levelhand shinglers, from 7s. to 12s. per day, or 35s. to 60s. per week; assistant shinglers, from 5s. to 7s. per day, or 25s. to 35s. per week; pullers-off, 3s. to 5s. per day, or 15s. to 25s. per week. The forge roller receives the blooms from the shinglers, and rolls the iron into bars of various widths. For this he is paid at the rate of 9d. to 1s. 4d. per ton (2400 lbs.). We pay one rate of 1s. per ton. Each roller employs helpers, and pays day wages. His income depends on the number of furnaces at work and quantity of iron rolled, and is not regular. The average will be about as follows:—Foremen rollers, from 6s. to 10s. per day, or 30s. to 50s. per week; assistant-rollers, from 4s. to 6s. per day, or 20s. to 30s. per week; young men assistants behind rolls, from 2s. 6d. to 3s. 6d. per day, or 12s. 6d. to 18s. per week; boys, from 1s. 6d. to 2s. per day, or 7s. 6d. to 10s. per week; hot bar drawers, from 3d. per ton, or 2s. 6d. to 5s. per day, or 12s. 6d. to 25s. per week; puddle bar weighers, 3d. per ton, or 4s. to 6s. per day, or 24s. to 30s. per week; cutters down, 4s. to 6s. per day, or 24s. to 30s. per week; assistants, 3s. to 4s. per day, or 18s. to 24s. per week; labourers, 2s. 6d. to 3s. per day, or 15s. to 18s. per week; foremen engine drivers, from 40s. to 50s.; assistant engine drivers, 25s. to 30s.; stokers or firemen, 18s. to 21s.; blacksmiths, 24s. to 30s., and even 35s.; blacksmiths' strikers, 16s. to 21s. per week; pig weighers, coal heavers, puddlers' tap wheelers,* 4s. to 5s. per day, or 24s. to 30s. per week.

Rate of wages paid for rolling, heating, and shearing sheet iron is as follows:—Sheet iron, 8 to 13 gauge, 10s. 6d.; 18 to

---

* These men do a large amount of work, fully equal to the average work of two labourers.

K

20 gauge, 12s. 6d.; 21 to 24 gauge, 16s.; 25 to 27 gauge, 19s. 6d., per ton of 2400 lbs. The daily or weekly earnings of this class also varies, being regulated by the class or thickness of sheets required. The average will be about as follows:— Foremen rollers (having charge of mill on both turns, day and night) from 15s. to 20s. per day, or 75s. to 100s. per week, and in some cases £6 per week; under rollers, paid by foreman, 10s. to 14s. per day, or 50s. to 70s. per week; rollers having charge of one turn only, 10s. to 16s. a day, or 50s. to 80s. per week; furnacemen (heaters), 7s. to 10s. per day, or 35s. to 50s. per week; shearers, 7s. to 10s. a day, or 35s. to 50s. per week; assistants behind rolls, 3s. 3d. to 4s. 6d. per day, or 16s. to 24s. per week; boys or youths, 1s. to 2s. 6d. per day, or 6s. to 15s. per week.

Plate rollers, furnacemen, shearers, and assistants.—The average income of this class depends upon the size, thickness, and weight of the plates, the number and size of the furnaces working in one mill, also to the number of rolls and the rolling mill arrangements. The mills in the South Staffordshire district are arranged to produce about 6 to 10 tons of boiler and tank plates during 12 hours. The mills in North Staffordshire and the North of England produce double the weight of ship and bridge plates during the same time. There is one mill at Stockton-on-Tees that has finished 360 tons of plates in one week. The following is about the rate paid and the average earnings of workmen in this district:—Plates to 3-16 in. thick, 7s. to 7s. 6d. per ton of 2400 lbs. Average wages:—Foremen rollers, 12s. to 20s. per day, or £3 to £5 per week; assistant rollers, 4s. to 6s. a day, or £1 to £1 10s per week; furnacemen, 7s. to 10s. per day, or £1 15s. to £2 10s. per week; assistants, 4s. to 6s. per day, or 20s. to 30s. per week; shearers, 10s. to 20s. per day, or 50s. to 100s. per week; assistant men and boys, 1s. 6d. to 5s. per day; men and boys behind rolls, 2s. to 5s. per day.

Stocktakers, or weighers of plates and sheets:—Foremen, 25s. to 35s. per week; assistants, 3s. to 4s. per day, or 18s. to 24s. per week; horse drivers and waggoners, 18s. to 21s. per week.

In the Pattern Makers the wages are reported as follows: —The average wages are 32s. per week of 54 hours. Workmen are paid 7d. per hour. There are no women employed in the trade. Apprentices' wages range from 3s. to 6s. for the first year per week, and rise to from 10s. to 12s. per week during the last year of their apprenticeship. Workmen receive full wages at the completion of their apprenticeship—viz., 21 years. There are very few workmen engaged upon piece-work. Their wages run at the rate of time and a half. The wages do not differ materially, excepting in different districts, and they are paid the same for every description of work, and at the rate of time and a quarter for overtime.

Workmen are employed $9\frac{1}{2}$ hours per day; $6\frac{1}{2}$ Saturdays—making 54 per week.

The tools used belong to the workmen. They cost at commencement from about £8 to £16, and about 6d. per week to keep up the stock.

The continuity of work depends a good deal upon circumstances. Some men have constant employment, while others work scarcely six months in the year, taking an average, deducting holidays, stoppages from breakdowns, &c., about ten months in the year. No time is lost by our workmen owing to inclement weather.

Wages in 1879 were the same as they are now. They have fluctuated considerably during that period. There have been two advances and as many reductions of wages.

SALT WORKS.

Sub-Order 5.

The wages of salt makers were given in the Miscellaneous Statistics for 1880 as follows:—Salt makers, men, 30s.; lads, 18s.; boatmen, men, 24s.; loaders, 24s.; smiths, men, 26s.; lads, 9s.; engine drivers, men, 26s.

APPENDIX.

PRICES PAID AT GREENWICH HOSPITAL

For food, clothing and household stores, and rates of artificers' wages, in the following years:—

Years.	Flesh.	Bread.	Flour.	Butter.	Cheese.	Beer.
	per cwt. £ s. d.	d. oz.	per cwt. £ s. d.	per lb. s. d.	per lb. s. d.	per barrel. £ s. d.
1740	1 8 0	1 per 9	..	0 5	0 8¼	0 5 2¾
1750	1 6 6	1 per 13	..	0 5½	0 3½	0 5 8¾
1760	1 11 6	..	..	0 5½	0 3¼	0 5 7¾
1770	1 8 6	1 per 11	..	0 6¼	0 3¾	0 5 10
1780	1 12 6	..	..	0 6¼	0 3¾	0 7 3½
1790	1 12 10	..	2 3 4	0 6½	0 4	0 8 7
1800	3 4 4	..	4 16 0	0 11¼	0 6½	1 0 4½
1810	3 12 0	..	4 8 4	1 1½	0 8½	0 17 10
1820	3 10 4½	1¾ per lb.	2 15 1	0 9½	0 7	0 13 10½
1830	2 3 6	..	2 14 11	0 6½	0 4	0 12 6½
1840	2 14 0	..	2 11 9½	0 10	0 4¾	0 14 3
1850	2 18 9	..	2 15 9	0 11½	0 8	1 4 5
1860	3 12 7	1¼ per lb.	1 18 3½	1 0	0 8	1 1 8
1865	2 17 5½	1½ per lb.	1 17 10	0 11¾	0 7½	1 4 8½

Years.	Candles.	Coal.	Carpenters and Joiners.	Bricklayers.	Masons.	Plumbers.
		per chaldr. £ s. d.				
1740	5/6	1 9 0	2/6 to 2/8	2/6	2/8	3/0
1750	6/2	1 7 7½	2/6 ,, 2/8	2/3	2/8	2/6
1760	6/10	1 12 8	2/6 ,, 2/8	2/6	2/8	2/6
1770	6/10¾	1 9 1½	2/6 ,, 2/8	2/4	2/8	3/0
1780	6/9½	1 17 3¾	2/6 ,, 2/8	2/4	2/10	3/0
1790	7/9	1 14 4¼	2/6 ,, 2/10	2/4	2/10	3/3
1800	10/4	2 11 7	2/10 ,, 3/2	3/0	2/10	3/3
1810	10/9¾	3 0 8	5/8 ,, 5/3	5/2	5/3	5/9
1820	8/2¾	2 5 9	5/3	5/1	5/3	5/9
1830	5/3½	1 7 0	5/6	4/9	5/5	5/6
1840	6/5½	0 19 8	5/5	4/10 to 4/8	5/3	5/5
1850	6/9	1 7 11	4/3	5/0	5/0	5/0
1860	6/3	0 17 9	4/8 to 5/0	4/8 to 5/0	4/8 to 5/0	5/0 to 5/6
1865	5/8	0 18 10	4/8 ,, 5/0	5/0	5/0	5/6

AVERAGE PRICES OF WHEAT, MEAT, POTATOES AND COAL.

From the Report of the Registrar-General of Births, Deaths, and Marriages in England.

Year.	Wheat.		Beef, Mean.	Mutton, Mean.	Best Seaham Coal in the London Market, per ton.		Best Potatoes at Waterside Market, Southwark per ton, Mean.		Annual Marriage Rate to 1000 Living.
	s.	d.	d.	d.	s.	d.	s.	d.	
1852	40	10	$4\frac{1}{8}$	$4\frac{7}{8}$	15	5	91	0	17·4
1853	52	11	$4\frac{7}{8}$	$5\frac{7}{8}$	20	1	130	6	17·9
1854	72	5	$5\frac{4}{8}$	$6\frac{7}{8}$	22	8	119	0	17·2
1855	74	8	$5\frac{6}{8}$	$5\frac{6}{8}$	20	10	100	6	16·2
1856	69	2	$5\frac{3}{8}$	$5\frac{6}{8}$	17	10	85	6	16·7
1857	56	5	$5\frac{3}{8}$	$5\frac{7}{8}$	17	7	120	6	16·5
1858	44	3	$5\frac{3}{8}$	$5\frac{6}{8}$	17	4	120	0	16·0
1859	43	10	$5\frac{4}{8}$	$5\frac{7}{8}$	17	3	94	0	17·0
1860	53	3	$5\frac{3}{8}$	$6\frac{1}{8}$	19	0	132	6	17·1
1861	55	4	$5\frac{3}{8}$	$6\frac{1}{8}$	18	5	124	0	16·3
1862	55	5	$5\frac{1}{8}$	$5\frac{7}{8}$	16	6	137	0	16·1
1863	44	8	$5\frac{3}{8}$	$5\frac{7}{8}$	17	1	100	6	16·8
1864	40	2	$5\frac{4}{8}$	$6\frac{3}{8}$	19	0	75	0	17·2
1865	41	9	$5\frac{6}{8}$	7	19	1	88	0	17·5
1866	49	11	$5\frac{7}{8}$	$6\frac{3}{8}$	19	0	89	0	17·5
1867	64	5	$5\frac{5}{8}$	6	19	8	138	0	16·5
1868	63	9	$5\frac{6}{8}$	$5\frac{6}{8}$	17	7	137	6	16·1
1869	48	2	$6\frac{1}{8}$	$6\frac{3}{8}$	17	8	99	6	15·9
1870	46	10	6	$6\frac{4}{8}$	17	5	104	6	16·1
1871	56	10	$6\frac{4}{8}$	7	18	2	77	6	16·7
1872	57	0	$6\frac{4}{8}$	$7\frac{3}{8}$	23	10	132	0	17·4
1873	58	8	7	$7\frac{4}{8}$	31	3	159	0	17·6
1874	55	8	$6\frac{6}{8}$	$6\frac{6}{8}$	24	8	111	0	17·0
1875	45	2	$6\frac{7}{8}$	$7\frac{3}{8}$	22	9	99	6	16·7
1876	46	2	$6\frac{5}{8}$	$7\frac{4}{8}$	20	2	—		16·5
1877	56	9	$6\frac{3}{8}$	7	18	5	146	0	15·7
1878	46	5	$5\frac{3}{8}$	$7\frac{1}{8}$	16	10	156	6	15·2
1879	43	10	$5\frac{6}{8}$	$6\frac{6}{8}$	16	11	157	9	14·4
1880	44	4	$6\frac{1}{8}$	$6\frac{7}{8}$	14	11	141	5	14·9
1881	45	4	$5\frac{7}{8}$	$7\frac{1}{8}$	16	0	—		15·1
1882	45	1	$6\frac{3}{8}$	$7\frac{1}{8}$	15	10	—		15·5

APPENDIX.

PURCHASE VALUE OF THE SOVEREIGN.

Quantities obtainable for One Pound Sterling.

	Flour.	Beef.	Butter.	Coal.
	lbs.	lbs.	lbs.	lbs.
1820	113	70	25	193
1825	112	61	23	185
1830	119	71	36	215
1835	194	70	32	215
1840	115	86	24	198
1845	151	93	26	247
1850	190	93	32	280
1855	103	42	28	215
1860	145	44	25	235
1865	183	41	21	234
1870	163	40	18	255
1875	170	34	19	197
1880	173	39	21	300

For flour, calculated on the average prices for the year.

For meat, from 1820 to 1855, from the Return of prices of grain, flour, &c., 264, of 1881, and subsequently from the average prices of beef given by the Registrar-General.

For butter, from the same Return.

For coal, from 1820 to 1850, from the Return 225, of 1881.

The prices taken are:—Meat, at the Metropolitan Meat Market, by the carcase; butter, from the prices paid by the Greenwich Hospital to 1850, and subsequently from declared value of imports of French butter; coal, from the annual average prices, exclusive of City or other dues, of the best coal at the ships' side in the Port of London.

PAUPERS IN ENGLAND AND WALES, IN QUINQUENNIAL AVERAGES.

Years.	Population.	Number of Adult Able-bodied	Per 1000	Number of all other Paupers.	Per 1000	Total Paupers.	Per 1000.
1849-53	18,000,000	154,173	8·5	709,647	39·3	869,820	48·3
1854-58	19,000,000	147,737	7·7	712,156	32·2	859,893	45·2
1859-63	20,000,000	169,170	8·4	769,090	38·4	938,144	46·9
1864-68	21,000.000	168,228	8·0	808,913	38·5	978,942	46·6
1869-73	22,000,000	169,709	7·7	843,467	38·3	1,013,135	46·0
1873-78	24,000,000	103,466	4·3	669,636	21·9	773,102	32·2
1879-83	26,000,000	113,593	4·3	694,087	26·6	807,680	34·9

APPENDIX.

AMOUNT OF DEPOSITS IN THE SAVINGS' BANKS.

Years.	Amount of Deposits.	Per head of Population.
	£	£ s. d.
1849—1853	38,215,000	2 2 2
1854—1858	43,578,000	2 5 2
1859—1863	50,828,000	2 11 0
1864—1868	47,011,000	2 5 0
1869—1873*	68,410,000	3 1 0
1874—1878*	80,814,000	3 7 4
1879—1883*	92,129,000	3 10 6

* Trustees and Post Office Savings' Banks united.

FRIENDLY SOCIETIES.

Year.	Number of Members.	Amount of Funds.
		£
1865	*1,374,425	5,362,072
1871	*1,560,886	8,062,894
1877	4,562,301	10,923,512
1879	4,650,754	12,741,171
1883	4,242,084	†8,550,355

* Number of Members not fully returned.
† Exclusive of branches with funds amounting to probably £4,000,000.

INDUSTRIAL AND CO-OPERATIVE SOCIETIES.

Year.	Number of Members.	Amount of Funds.
		£
1865	148,286	1,017,106
1870	249,113	2,231,389
1875	420,024	5,220,011
1880	526,686	5,806,545
1883	572,610	8,200,722

BUILDING SOCIETIES.

Year.	Amount of Funds.
1875	£11,703,926
1879	31,164,178
1883	48,938,320

RANKEN AND Co., Printers, Drury House, Drury Court, Strand, London, W.C.

www.ingramcontent.com/pod-product-compliance
Lightning Source LLC
Chambersburg PA
CBHW030314170426
43202CB00009B/1000